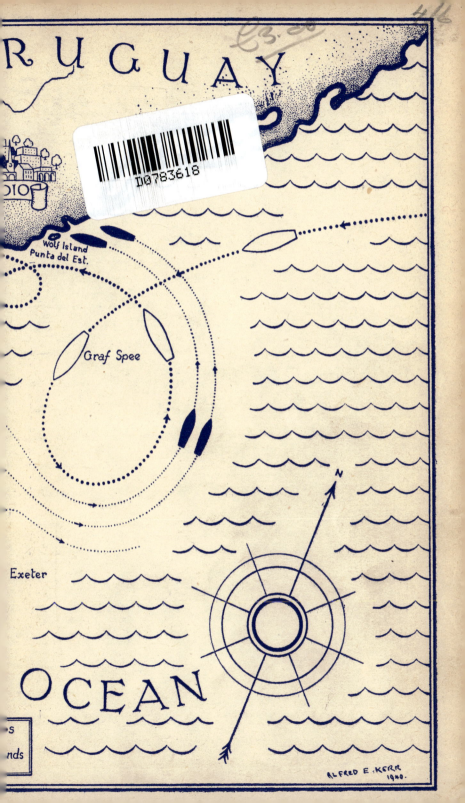

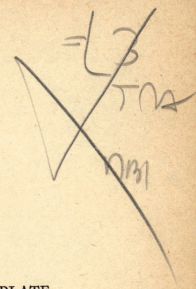

THE BATTLE OF THE PLATE

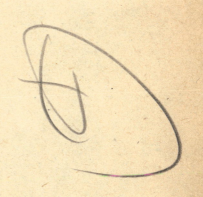

INTERNAL EXPLOSIONS BREAK THE BACK OF THE RAIDER.

THE BATTLE OF THE PLATE

by

COMDR. A. B. CAMPBELL, R.D.

With a Foreword by

THE RT. HON. LORD CHATFIELD,
P.C., G.C.B., O.M., K.C.M.G., C.V.O.,
ADMIRAL OF THE FLEET

HERBERT   JENKINS   LIMITED
3 DUKE OF YORK STREET ST. JAMES'S
LONDON, S.W.1

Published	.	.	.	.	May	1940
Reprinted	.	.	.	.	May	1940
Reprinted	.	.	.	.	August	1940
Reprinted	.	.	.	.	November	1940
Reprinted	.	.	.	.	April	1941
Reprinted	.	.	.	.	September	1941

Printed in Great Britain by
Wyman & Sons, Ltd., London, Fakenham and Reading.

CONTENTS

ILLUSTRATIONS

FOREWORD

By the RT. HON. LORD CHATFIELD,
P.C., G.C.B., O.M., K.C.M.G., C.V.O.,
ADMIRAL OF THE FLEET

IN this Island home of ours it is impossible to get more than seventy miles from the sea. No wonder then that we have the taste of the salt on our lips. But the fact that we live on an island involves both a risk and a safeguard. Much of our food and raw materials must be carried by our ships from overseas and herein lies the danger. Our trade routes must be kept open for these ships and this is one of the duties that falls on our Navy. Remember that there are over 85,000 miles of these routes, and you will realize what a tremendous task is before them. As one of Kipling's characters said about our merchant vessels: "And if anyone hinders our coming you'll starve."

This is a story of the raider that harassed our ships, sinking them and making their crews prisoners, and of the manner in which the Royal Navy rounded her up and brought her successfully to action. Commodore Harwood's action off the River Plate has thrilled the people of these Islands as did in their day the exploits of the great sea captains of the past. It is a story that, as Mr. Churchill has said, "will live long in song and story."

I recommend this book to everyone who delights in hearing of the work of the British Navy, for the incidents here recorded add another leaf to its laurels.

AUTHOR'S PREFACE

THE story of the Battle of the Plate is an
object lesson to all Britons. If the British
Empire is to exist it is vital that it should hold
the command of the seas. The fact that an
enemy commerce raider was accounted for when
the *Graf Spee* was scuttled after defeat by British
cruisers had an immediate reaction in this
country. Within a fortnight the butter ration
was doubled. This meant that ships which
had been held up in foreign ports were able to
sail more freely. Command of the seas does not
mean simply driving our enemies off them, it
means keeping the trade routes open to our
ships and locking those of our enemies in harbour
so that they are unable to take foodstuffs and
vital raw materials to their people.

So the command of the seas may still be
maintained though a big naval action is never
fought. It is the might of the British Navy that
keeps the enemy in his harbours, and but for this
might we could never have landed an army in
France without loss. The man in the street is apt
to take the transport of a British expeditionary

force for granted, but a moment's thought will convince him of the magnitude of the operation and the command of the seas that its success implies. Further, we could not keep our munition factories working as they are if our merchantmen had not brought materials safely from all parts of the world.

In September, 1939, German liners and cargo ships were scattered all over the world in the ordinary course of their lawful occasions. When war was declared on September 3rd they ran for shelter to the nearest neutral port and there they will remain until the end of the war. Why did they cease operating? For the simple reason that they dare not sail lest they should meet a British cruiser, who would promptly capture them and confiscate their cargoes. They knew that they might expect to encounter British ships in all parts of the world, so vast is our maritime power.

What of our own merchantmen? They carried on as usual, for they knew that there were but few German ships on the high seas and they felt that the British Navy was ready to cope with them.

We now know that there was one German ship that was causing a great deal of trouble, and this book tells of how the British Navy ran her off the seas. This particular ship was built especially as a commerce raider. She had sunk nine of our merchant ships before she was driven to defeat. The enemy has several such raiders. We know that the *Graf Spee* has two sister-ships who could effect the same amount of damage to peaceful merchantmen, but they dare not come out. It is the might of our Navy that keeps them skulking in port. They might manage to evade our Northern Patrol, for the sea is a very wide space and it is not a difficult feat to slip through when darkness and foul weather are on your side. But even if they did get into the wide seas they have no support from their own Navy and their end would be as inglorious as was that of the *Graf Spee*.

It seems fitting that our New Zealand Dominion should have sent a ship that was instrumental in assisting at the sinking of this raider, for in the last war it was her sister dominion, Australia, that sent the ship which accounted for the *Emden*, a raider that did a deal of destruction in the Indian Ocean before being sunk at the Cocos Islands by H.M.A.S. *Sydney*. New Zealand has cause to be proud of H.M.S. *Achilles*.

It was not until three months after the outbreak of war that the activities of our far-flung Navy came into the public ken. Then people began to ask what the South American Division was doing. These ships were part of our America and West Indies Station and were joined at outbreak of war by *Achilles* from New Zealand.

The British Navy covers the world. Naturally the biggest fleet is the Home Fleet, which operates from home waters to the rock of Gibraltar. Then there is the Mediterranean Fleet, and still further east the East Indies Station, which also patrols the Persian Gulf and the Red Sea. Still further east is the China Station based on Hong Kong. Australia and New Zealand have their own navies. Canada maintains ships in the Atlantic and the Pacific and there is the Royal Indian Marine, so our trade routes are well policed.

It might be asked why do the Germans not come out and attack trade ships nearer home. The reason is that they are aware that to-day, before they could even get near the Channel, our fleet would be out to give them battle. So in effect they surrender the command of the seas by their passivity.

Britain has two navies, the navy of defence and the navy of supply, and both are vital to our national life. I like to think that the navy of defence—the Royal Navy—is the suit of mail. It is kept bright and sound and is a sure shield, but of what use is a suit of mail without a man inside? The navy of supply—the Merchant Service—is the man inside, and when these two services work together, as they do, then this nation will continue to rule the waves and in so doing bring sanity and reason back into a world that has gone mad.

In writing this account of the Battle of the Plate so soon after its occurrence I have had to rely to a great extent on accounts given to me by eyewitnesses. I have found some difficulty in reconciling their descriptions, but this is quite understandable. In the heat of battle there is not much time or opportunity for observing the movements of other ships; the enemy is the main objective.

My knowledge of the conditions and climate of South America, gained when on naval patrol in that part during the Great War, has enabled me to place the setting accurately.

The "hush-hush" policy of governments to-day has not made my task any easier. Every atom of information that might possibly be of value to the enemy is suppressed, with the result that although I have told the story in what I believe to be its true perspective it may happen that at some future date slight modifications or revisions may be necessary.

One fact that stands out in the action is that the shooting on both sides was magnificent, proving that fire-control to-day is far in advance of that in the Great War.

I have tried to show that command of the seas goes to the nation that is ready to fight for it, and we *are and must continue to be that nation.*

In a book of this length it is impossible to do justice to the courage and splendid spirit of all who fought. Heroes all. I have recounted only some of the deeds of some of the men. These were honoured with decorations by His Majesty the King, but those who wear them will be the first to admit that the honour belongs to their shipmates as much as to themselves.

I would like to thank all those who have assisted me with information, especially the shipping companies who were concerned, and Captain J. Robison, of the *Newton Beech*, who was in the raider during the action, Captain F. C. P. Harris of the *Clement* and Captain W. B. Starr, of the *Tairoa*; also Ldg. Sig. Swanston and Ldg. Sto. J. H. Redmond and all the other good fellows, my brothers of the sea, with whom I talked. They all told me their story, but it was hard work extracting it, for, like all sailors, when I asked them they simply said: "Well, there isn't much to tell."

My friend Cecil Hunt has been of very great help He has been a perfect tyrant and I thank him.

I am also extremely grateful to Lord Chatfield for sponsoring this book.

To those who lost dear ones in the Battle of the Plate I offer my sincere sympathy. I salute their memory; both friend and foe.

One and all they died for their country and "Their Name Liveth for Evermore!"

A. B. CAMPBELL.

Adelphi, W.C.
    April, 1940.

THE BATTLE OF THE PLATE

CHAPTER I

THE HUNTERS

ON the 12th of December, 1939, H.M.S. *Exeter* was steaming swiftly and almost silently through the waters of the South Atlantic Ocean. She was lean and long, and the salt which caked her funnels and upper works gave evidence of grim battles with Atlantic storms.

It was in August, 1937, that Captain H. H. Harwood, O.B.E., was appointed to the South American Division of the West Indies Station, with the rank of Commodore 2nd Class while commanding, and temporarily with the rank of Commodore 1st Class during the absence through illness of Vice-Admiral S. J. Meyrick, C.B. H.M.S. *Exeter* became his flagship.

The multifarious peace-time duties of H.M.S. *Exeter* had included a visit to Valparaiso which coincided with the earthquake at Concepcion. On that occasion she was accompanied by H.M.S. *Ajax*, and they were able to accomplish such magnificent rescue work that Chileans declared the words *Exeter* and *Ajax* would be for ever engraved on their hearts.

H.M.S. *Exeter* and H.M.S. *Ajax* were still together in December, 1939, not within sight of each other, but in close communication by radio. They were also in touch with H.M.S. *Achilles* which had been loaned from the New Zealand Squadron at the outbreak of war with Nazi Germany on September 3, 1939.

The task of this trio was no easy one. It was their function to keep clear the vital trade routes so that the food supplies of Britain and her Allies should be unmolested.

Great Britain is the centre of the land surface of the globe. If you put one point of the compasses on London and with the other on Pekin describe a circle, you will have immediate proof. But being a small island, Britain is largely dependent for her food supplies upon overseas sources. Most of it comes from the east and west and, because it often does not pay cargo steamers to utilize the Panama or Suez Canals, the traffic comes round Cape Horn or the Cape of Good Hope.

The two main lines of trade routes converge at the entrance to the English Channel, where they are joined by the Western Ocean routes from Canada and the United States.

In war-time the function of a British naval patrol is to keep these vital trade arteries clear of enemy raiders. Merchant ships with food for Britain invariably receive sealed orders to join convoys which sail from the chief ports within the areas in which enemy raiders or submarines are expected to operate.

The convoy system clearly cannot be extended to all oceans, and fully loaded merchantmen must make their way at their own risk to these main ports before they can receive the protection of accompanying armed ships.

It is on these preliminary journeys that they are vulnerable. The raiders take good care to keep away from the convoyed areas and pursue their highwayman tactics in more distant waters. The British patrol has to act as policeman in these vast areas. Their "beat" is enormous; Britain has 85,000 miles of trade routes to protect, and patrolling them is one of the loneliest jobs on which a ship can be employed. There are few chances for the crew to get ashore and the men are subjected to a wide range of climate. The South Atlantic stretches from the Equator to the Antarctic Ocean and the area patrolled by the South American Division of the West Indies Station extended from the tropic of Capricorn to the southern extremities of South Africa and South America.

In war-time the activities of these patrol ships acquire a new significance. Almost from the outbreak of war it was apparent that an enemy raider of considerable size was operating in the boundless wastes of the South Atlantic. The vast area involved was splendidly suited to its tip-and-run tactics which were soon responsible for the loss of several unarmed British merchantmen. The conditions equally made its apprehension a difficult task.

H.M.S. *Exeter* is one of the "Town" class of light cruisers. She is long and low-lying and built for speed. She can work up swiftly to 30 knots. Her length is 576 ft., her beam 57 ft. Her draught is only 17 ft., for in searching for enemy raiders such ships have frequently to steam up uncharted channels and inlets which a greater draught would make unnavigable. The gross tonnage of H.M.S. *Exeter* is 8,390. She is camouflaged a dull grey to make her less conspicuous against her own element, the sea, and to break up identifying lines and details which can be picked out from a distance. She has a main armament of six 8-in. guns. Their shells weigh 256 pounds and have a range of 14 miles. These 8-in. guns protrude from three turrets on her deck. The turrets are placed amidships so that the guns can be fired on either port or starboard side without turning the ship. These 8-in. guns are a very heavy armament for so light a ship.

H.M.S. *Exeter* also has a secondary battery of four 4-in. anti-aircraft guns which have proved of immense value since attack from the air became an important part of naval warfare. She has two aircraft ready in their catapults on deck. Her full complement is 600 men.

Her officers were men of wide experience and considerable achievement and had had the advantage of a long term in the ship, which means much in the perfection of team work. Before Commodore Harwood made *Exeter* his flagship in 1936 he had had two years on the staff of the Royal Naval War College, before which he was in command of H.M.S. *London* as Flag Captain in the First Cruiser Squadron. During the Great War, before which Commodore Harwood had specialized in torpedoes, he was Torpedo Officer to the cruiser *Sutlej* and to the battleship *Royal Sovereign*. From 1922 for four years he served at the Admiralty in the Plans Division. He is a fluent Spanish scholar. see p 332 Dudley Pope

Captain F. S. Bell was promoted to Captain as recently as 1938. He joined the Royal Navy in 1910 and went straight from Dartmouth to sea in 1914. He was a midshipman in the cruisers *Cumberland* and *Challenger* at the Cameroons. In 1915 he was in H.M.S. *Canada* in the Grand Fleet and was then selected to specialize in submarines, which branch of naval warfare occupied him until 1923. Captain Bell was subsequently lent to the Australian Navy and, in 1933, qualified for the Staff College. Two years later and until just before his promotion to Captain, he was Commander of the battle cruiser *Repulse*.

In the summer of 1939 Commodore Harwood transferred his broad pennant to H.M.S. *Ajax*.

H.M.S. *Ajax* is 520 ft. long, with a beam of 55 ft. and a draught of only 15 ft. 6 ins. Her gross tonnage is 6,985. She also is camouflaged but her armaments are less than those of *Exeter*. She carries eight 6-in. guns instead of six 8-in. guns. The projectile of the 6-in. gun weighs about 100 pounds. She has secondary batteries of anti-aircraft guns and two aircraft that can be catapulted from her decks. Her officers and crew number 522.

She is commanded by Captain C. H. L. Woodhouse, who entered the Navy in 1906 and secured firsts in all subjects in passing as Lieutenant. During the Great War he was Sub-Lieutenant and Lieutenant in H.M.S. *Bristol*, and was in action off the Falkland Islands against the German China Squadron under the command of Admiral Graf von Spee. From 1915 to 1918 Lieutenant Woodhouse specialized in gunnery and served with the Malaya Grand Fleet. He was promoted to Commander in

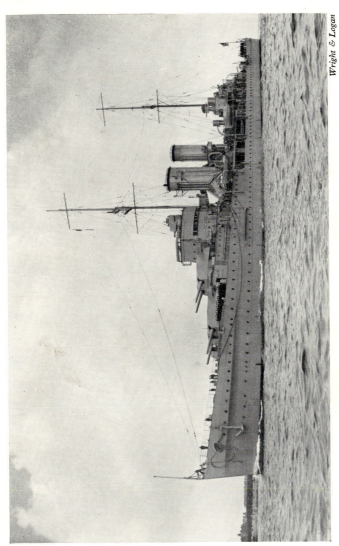

Wright & Logan

H.M.S. "EXETER" WITH HER DISTINGUISHING TALL MASTS.

1927 and Captain in 1934. Four years previously he had qualified as a Staff Officer, and before appointment to command H.M.S. *Ajax* on the American Station in October, 1937, he was for two years Assistant Director of Naval Equipment.

The third ship of the trio, H.M.S. *Achilles*, is practically a sister ship. Her length is 522 ft., her beam 55 ft. and her draught 16 ft. Her camouflage cannot completely hide her weighty armaments. Like *Ajax* she has eight 6-in. guns, a secondary armament of anti-aircraft guns but only one catapulted aircraft on deck. She has a complement of 550.

In 1933 she established a world record for long-distance speeding at high speed by a warship of her class. She travelled 1,100 nautical miles in 39 hours, maintaining an average of 29 knots, and did not force her engines in any way during this remarkable run.

In January, 1939, Captain W. E. Parry was appointed to the command of the *Achilles*. He joined the Royal Navy in 1905 and passed out head of his term of cadets at Dartmouth, gaining five firsts in his Lieutenant tests. He is a torpedo specialist and was Torpedo Officer of H.M.S. *Birmingham* in the Grand Fleet during the Great War. From 1932 to 1935 he was Executive Officer of the aircraft carrier

Eagle in China, and for the two next years was Commander of the Anti-Submarine Establishment at Portland. During 1938 Captain Parry took a course at the Imperial Defence College and from there proceeded to H.M.S. *Achilles* which had been lent to the New Zealand Government and was a training ship for New Zealand ratings.

At the outbreak of war H.M.S. *Achilles* was loaned to the South American Squadron. Her crew included 327 New Zealanders and she immediately made contact with H.M.S. *Exeter* and H.M.S. *Ajax*, and achieved with them the co-operation and co-ordination under Commodore Harwood which were to prove of such value in their search for the enemy raider.

CHAPTER II

THE LION AND THE JACKAL

O N September 30, 1939, the South Atlantic was a sheet of glass and the sky overhead looked like a vast steel dome. The tropic sun poured down upon the decks of s.s. *Clement* as she steamed slowly along the Brazilian coast off the port of Bahia. She was an ocean-going tramp steamer, a doughty veteran. This class of vessel, with no pretence to comeliness, is a vital link in the supply of food and raw materials to Britain's cities and towns. Her anchor flukes probably still bore the mud of the Yangtsze River, and her sides showed scratches and scrapes caused by lying alongside busy wharves in all parts of the world. She was a vessel of 5,000-odd tons belonging to the Booth Line, and commanded by Captain F. C. P. Harris. She had a speed of 15 knots and was a typical "tubby" ocean-going tramp.

There were many experienced seamen among her crew and they were prepared by the first weeks of the war to find that their normally peaceful occasions were likely to be harassed.

They knew, in fact, that no trade route was safe from enemy raiders and that at any moment they might have to face risks that more legitimately belonged to the fighting services.

Nevertheless, the sudden appearance of a warship off the port bow did not give rise to immediate alarm. In his personal account of the happenings of that eventful morning Captain Harris wrote:

"At about 11.10 a.m. on September 30, after getting the sun on the meridian to check the latitude, I left the bridge for a few minutes, telling the Third Officer, who was on watch, to call me at once if he sighted anything. For some time we had been zigzagging as I had been informed that although no enemy submarines had been reported, they might be expected at any time. Of course, we had no gun and only our speed to protect us.

"About ten minutes later the Third Officer called me by voice-tube and told me a man-of-war was bearing down on us, about four points on the port bow.

"I thought it was probably H.M.S. *Ajax*, as I had been on board her a few weeks before in Pará and expected her to be somewhere about.

"I went up on the bridge and had a look at her with the glass, but as she was dead end on to us I could make nothing out about her except that by the huge bow waves she was apparently closing us at great speed.

"I told the Third Officer to have the Ensign put up and went to my room for a few minutes and put on a clean white uniform jacket.

"When I next went on to the bridge the man-of-war was about four miles off and still coming in fast, but I could make nothing of her. I couldn't see her flag and she had no signals flying.

"A few minutes later a seaplane zoomed over us. This didn't worry me at all as I knew the *Ajax* had one. The Chief Officer came running up and asked should he show our name board. I consented. Then the 'plane flew over us again and sprayed the bridge with bullets from a machine-gun. I immediately stopped engines. It was then seen that the 'plane had German markings under the wings.

"'My God!' said Mr. Jones, the Chief Officer, 'it's a Jerry. Shall I get the boats ready, sir?'

"'Yes,' I said. 'Get all hands on deck and swing them out.'

"Three or four times more the 'plane passed over us, spraying the boat-deck and bridge with bullets, although the ship was stopped. The bullets fell around me on the bridge and round the men on the boat-deck like hail. I can't

31

understand to this day why some of us were not killed.

"I had got the Wireless Officer to send out an S O S with our position, which message he informed me had been picked up and answered by a Brazilian steamer.

"After getting rid of all confidential papers and documents and doing everything necessary about the bridge, I went down on to the boat-deck where I found that everything was going along in true boat-drill fashion and that nearly all the boats were in the water. The only person wounded as far as I could see was the Chief Officer, and he had blood on his right hand and forearm where two bullets had struck him.

"The battleship by this time had rounded-to about half a mile on our port beam with her guns trained on us and, taking it for granted from the machine-gun fire from the 'plane that they intended to sink the *Clement* as soon as possible and wanted us to clear out, I gave orders to abandon ship.

"When we were all in the boats a piquet boat bore down on us and took the Chief Engineer and myself on board. The boat then proceeded on to the *Clement* and a sack full of bombs were placed on board. The Chief Engineer and I were taken on board the battleship.

"On the way the officer in charge of the piquet

boat told us all to put on life-jackets as the
Clement would blow up and might blow the
piquet boat out of the water. But those bombs
never exploded.

"On passing under the stern of the battleship
I saw the embossed letters on her quarter,
Admiral Scheer, which, of course, had been
painted over with grey paint.

"When we stepped out of the piquet boat
on board the battleship the Chief Engineer
and I were escorted up to the bridge where
we met the Captain who saluted in true naval
fashion and said, after shaking my hand: 'I am
sorry, Captain, but I will have to sink your
ship. It is war.'

"Then two torpedoes were fired at the *Clement*
but both missed, one passing ahead and the
other passing astern although both ships were
stopped dead and there was practically no
swell. She was eventually sunk by gunfire,
and it took about 25 rounds of 6-in. and 5 rounds
of 11-in."

The German Commander impressed Captain
Harris as a fine sailor of the best type, who had
a hearty distaste for the predatory activities
he was called upon to perform.

"I don't want to fight," he once volunteered
to Captain Harris, "and *you* don't want to
fight, so what is the use of it all?" he said.

The man's innate decency would not be hidden and was in shining contrast to the ruthlessness displayed by other Nazi commanders from the very first day of the war. It is doubtful, knowing Langsdorff's record, that he authorized, or was even aware of, the machine-gunning of the *Clement* by the gunner of the catapulted 'plane that had first spotted the victim, especially as the British master had made no show of useless resistance.

Captain Hans Langsdorff was a typical German naval officer of the old Imperial régime. He was a man of forty-two years of age—young to be the Captain of one of Germany's pocket battleships—he had served for twenty-seven years in the Navy and was a cadet on board the *Groser Kurfurest* in the Great War, taking part in the Battle of Jutland. The phrase "the brotherhood of the sea" was no idle tinkle of words to him; he believed in that brotherhood and fulfilled its highest obligations.

The two British prisoners were accorded treatment and accommodation appropriate to their rank and soon had opportunity to appreciate that the pocket battleship was the essence of ingenuity and scientific efficiency.

They were not, of course, permitted to probe any of the much-vaunted secrets of the battleship but they had ample opportunity to assess her main features. Like her two sister-ships the *Deutschland* and *Von Scheer*, the *Graf Spee* was reputed to embody many remarkable new inventions, the chief aim of their designers being to combine the power, speed and wide cruising range so necessary to the lone raider. Captain Langsdorff often claimed that his ship was "faster than every more powerful ship and more powerful than every faster ship." But this claim was born of policy rather than conviction, for in the privacy of his own cabin he admitted on several occasions to the existence of British and French battle cruisers which could both outpace and outrange his own vessel.

The *Graf Spee* had a gross tonnage of 10,000 tons. She was 690 ft. long, had a 70-ft. beam and a draught of 22 ft. Her full complement was 926 officers and men.

The British merchantmen, seeing the crew at work, were struck by the extreme youth of the majority of the ship's company. Most of the officers were seasoned men and naval reserve officers, but the crew seemed to average between eighteen to twenty-three years. They looked unduly youthful for such work, but they were quite friendly towards the captives.

The main armaments consisted of six 11-in. guns, each firing a projectile of 670 pounds.

35

She was thus able to hurl a broadside of 4,700 pounds of steel and high explosives.

Her secondary armament was eight 5.9-in. guns, six 4.1-in. anti-aircraft guns, and eight 3-pounders. She carried two aircraft which could be catapulted from her decks and were invaluable as extra eyes for the raider. Without them her visual range would have been limited to twenty miles; with them every ship within 1,500 miles was liable to detection.

The British master did not have long to wait in order to appreciate the remarkable speed of this ship. Captain Langsdorff had no intention of being near the scene of the sinking of the *Clement* when her crew was picked up. Although no British ships were near enough to be visible there was always the possibility that his enemy might have intercepted the wireless message from the *Clement*. Actually the speed of the *Graf Spee* was 26 knots, but, what was even more vital to her purpose as a raider, she had an economic cruising speed of 15 knots over the enormous range of 10,000 miles.

About five hours after Captain Langsdorff had taken the British Master and his Chief Engineer aboard he contacted a neutral ship which proved to be of Greek ownership. She was stopped and an officer sent aboard.

The two captives were transferred, and, as Captain Harris continued:

"We were nine days on the Greek steamer getting to St. Vincent. Everyone aboard was very kind to us and wanted to carry us to England, but in all my forty-five years of sea-going I have never travelled on such a dirty ship. The paintwork and decks, even the floors of the rooms and saloon, were covered with coal dust from the last time of coaling. We were thankful to reach St. Vincent.

"There the British Consul took us under his wing and put us up in his own home where we were most comfortable. We were seventeen days there before we could get a ship to take us home. Eventually the Dutch steamer *Amstelkirk* agreed to give us a passage, and nine days later we landed at Havre. That night we caught the Southampton steamer and after a rough passage landed on Sunday, November 5.

"All I had to wear was a pair of flannel trousers and a sports jacket given me in St. Vincent by a passenger on a steamer that was passing through. I had no hat as I couldn't get one to fit me at St. Vincent, and no overcoat. It is a drawback sometimes to be generously built."

Meantime the German Commander was thinking not of the past but of future prisoners. Every day at dawn the eyes of the raider were launched from her decks. For two or three hours the aeroplanes hovered and circled above the ship, reporting from their high altitude the best prospects for the raider.

It was clear from his boasts to British captains that the German Commander was well informed as to the movements of British cargo vessels, particularly those whose routes he might be able to cross.

It transpired that he was frequently able to supplement and correct his information by the shipping columns of overseas newspapers found on board his victims. It was not long before British Masters were alive to this source of information and they made a point of sinking all such publications at the same time as the confidential papers and code book were dropped overboard in a specially weighted bag when the raider was identified.

Raiding on the high seas is the modern equivalent of Dick Turpin's activities. In the old days of sailing ships the course was decided in a great measure by daily weather conditions. Ships had their objectives but could not forecast how they would reach them, neither could a raider searching for them know with any certainty where her victims were likely to be found. To-day, with mechanical propulsion, the trade routes are as clearly defined as the modern main-line railways. Even in war-time the considerations of time and fuel economy demand that these routes shall be adhered to. A raiding vessel cannot take cover, her only ruse is to keep out of sight but within the area of detection by hydrophone, and to rely upon her superior speed to molest any victim within her range.

On board the *Graf Spee*, in addition to the men straining their ears for the detecting notes of the hydrophone which can pick up the thud of a propeller for fifty miles or more, and ascertain its direction at the same time, there were double look-outs and gun crews standing at their stations ready for immediate action. The anti-aircraft guns were never left and the sound detectors, the great ears of the ship, were tuned to pick up the note of any approaching aircraft.

Then, on October 5, in the morning watch, the look-out reported another potential victim.

Immediately the order "General Quarters" was given, all routine work ceased. Stewards hastened to the sick bays, cooks left their galleys and joined up with the stretcher parties, ammunition hoists were opened up, fire parties bent the hose-pipes on to the cocks, and in a few moments everyone was at his battle station and the *Graf Spee* was transformed into a tense fighting unit.

Such feverish activity is the immediate result of sighting any ship, and not until her identity has been established is the "Carry On" given and the men relax to their normal duties.

In this case the vessel sighted was the *Newton Beech*, a vessel of nearly 3,000 tons, owned by Ridley Son and Tully of Newcastle-on-Tyne, and commanded by Captain J. Robison of South Shields. He and his officers were hoping they would be back in time to spend Christmas leave in England.

Their ship was a typical single-deck tramp vessel about 375 ft. in length and coal burning. She had a crew of thirty-four, of whom eight were deck- and engine-room officers, and she carried a wireless operator. Such ships rove the world and are sometimes away from their home ports for three, six, nine or even twelve months.

The *Newton Beech* had been adopted by the Burford St. Senior C.C. School at Hoddesdon, Herts, under the British Ship Adoption Society's scheme, and a considerable correspondence had taken place between the officers and men and the pupils of the school. This splendid scheme keeps youngsters at home in touch with our men on the high seas and the pupils delight in having a ship which they feel really belongs to them. This adoption scheme does much to lighten the monotonous life of the men of our tramp steamers, and enables youngsters to get to know the world in an entertaining and instructive fashion.

She was carrying a cargo of maize from Cape Town to Great Britain, but her experienced Captain knew that the uselessness of his cargo from a store point of view would not make him immune from the depredations of a raider.

How he was soon to be challenged by the German battleship is best told in his words in a letter written on January 31 to the school in which he and his men had so much interest:

"Since my last letter was written, many things have happened, first the war and then the sinking of my ship by enemy action, therefore the *Newton Beech* is no more, and I shall endeavour in as few words as possible to describe our experience.

"We sailed from the River Tyne in ballast on 5th August, and after an uneventful voyage arrived at Cape Town on 3rd September, the day Great Britain and France declared war against Germany.

"We were twenty-three days at Cape Town owing to the port being congested; this was owing to the Mediterranean being closed to British shipping at that time. While we were waiting there the vessel was fitted with a 4-in. gun and the officers and sailors were trained to man it.

"It was the 26th September when we sailed from Cape Town with a cargo of maize consisting of 7,080 tons, bound for the U.K., our port of call being Sierra Leone for orders and bunkers.

"At 6.0 a.m. on 5th October the Chief Officer awoke me and informed me that a man-of-war was overtaking us in such a direction that he could not make out the nationality of it. The weather was fine and warm and I went up on the bridge in my pyjamas, but the vessel was still about six miles away so therefore thought it prudent to put on some clothes. Afterwards we still could not make out the nationality but knew it was not British and became very suspicious. To be on the safe side we had the Radio Officer standing by to send out the required signal to other ships that might be in the vicinity, and I dumped my secret documents overboard, as these would have been of very great value to the enemy.

"When the vessel was almost abeam with her guns and torpedoes pointing at us, we sent out our radio message, having recognized her as the German battleship *Admiral Graf Spee*. The reason that we could not recognize her ensign sooner was owing to the ensign being frayed away so much that there was only one foot remaining, and it answered their purpose very well. We managed to send three radio messages out, which apparently were never heard by any vessel. Then the *Graf Spee* signalled to us to stop the radio or they would open fire. We made no attempt to use our gun, as it would have been foolhardy to do so. We were then ordered to heave-to and an armed prize crew boarded us, then we steamed around with the *Graf Spee* never out of sight.

"While in conversation with the German officers I mentioned that I was not surprised to see them as I had heard over the London broadcast that the *Graf Spee* had sunk the British vessel *Clement* a few days previously.

"This was an untruth on my part as the B.B.C. gave the name of the raider as the *Von Scheer*. The German officers denied all knowledge of the *Clement* but must have signalled this information to the Captain of the *Graf Spee*, for next day a motor boat came alongside and I was ordered to go and interview the Captain. When I shook hands with Captain Langsdorff he immediately said that his officers had informed him of what I had stated. I stuck to my story and then he admitted that they had indeed sunk the *Clement*."

When a raider's party boards a ship the officer in command goes to the bridge and demands of the Captain to see the ship's papers.

Meantime the firing party has taken up its position under the bridge with rifles at the ready. The Captain has no option but to comply.

The ship's papers of a merchantman on ocean-going trade are three. The Bill of Health testifies to the health of the crew and the absence of contagious or infectious disease at their last port of call. This bill is attached to the Clearance, which document records the port the ship has last left, the port she is making for and the fact that she has paid all dock fees and charges before leaving. Thirdly, and most important from a contraband point of view, is the Ship's Manifest. This is a complete list of all cargo carried, with the contents of each package, destination of the cargo and its disposition in the ship.

In the case of a boarding party searching for contraband this Manifest is a vital document, and the boarding party would be at liberty to demand that cases and holds be opened up at their direction to satisfy them that the cargo was in fact exactly as detailed on the Manifest. The leader of the boarding party in the *Newton Beech* had little interest in Captain Robison's cargo of maize.

The second officer of the boarding party would be examining the ship's stores with a special eye to fuel before deciding whether to transfer her assets before sinking her.

The *Graf Spee* had to fuel and victual for a 10,000-mile run and her stores were precious. Captain Langsdorff preferred his victims to be self-supporting; no doubt he had visions of other captures and indeed he was soon to find a further victim.

Two days later, on October 7 at 8.30 in the morning watch, Captain C. Pottinger of Bath, who commanded the *Ashlea*, a vessel of 4,200 tons, sighted a warship ten miles off the port beam. He did not expect to encounter a German battleship in that part of the world, and assumed that the stranger was a French vessel. Captain Pottinger did not use his radio as he thought the approaching warship would come close enough for visual signalling. So she did. But imagine his surprise when she broke her flag at the stern to find the German swastika fluttering before him.

The *Ashlea*, which was owned by the Clifford Shipping Co., Ltd., Newcastle-on-Tyne, was promptly signalled to heave-to. The towering bulk of the huge battleship made immediate compliance inevitable. Captain Pottinger reflected on his fate. He knew the enemy technique. There was little chance for the survival of his ship, although he discerned what was clearly a British tramp steamer in the wake of the battleship. Perhaps the raider was collecting prizes. The British skipper was not left long in doubt.

A boat was sent from the battleship and took off thirty-five of his crew to the *Newton Beech*, which they found on arrival to be manned by an armed German prize crew. The *Newton Beech* had for the moment become Captain Langsdorff's "annexe."

Captain Pottinger was transferred to the battleship herself and he had scarcely been able to realize his surroundings when there was a terrific explosion and a sheet of flame. The Germans had hung four time bombs over the sides of his ship. Six minutes later the *Ashlea* bulged out like a blown can and then turned slowly on to her beam ends. In the swirl of water as the suction increased the wreckage of her top hamper could be seen. The surface was strewn with shattered timbers, rafts and cases of stores.

On the next day the *Graf Spee* ordered the *Newton Beech* to stand by and her prisoners were then transferred by launch to the raider. Almost as soon as they had reached her decks the British seamen saw the gun crews in action. With a series of deafening reports shells from the 5.9's sank the *Newton Beech*.

THE GERMAN RAIDER UNDER WAY. THE FORE TURRET WITH ITS THREE
11-IN. GUNS IS CONSPICUOUS. THERE IS A SIMILAR TURRET AFT.

Those who watched her sinking counted themselves lucky to have their lives, but much that was irreplaceable disappeared before their eyes. The skipper had been nine years aboard her. He and his officers and men felt that she was part of their existence. For them it was a heartbreaking moment. They turned away and resigned themselves to the distraction of their new surroundings.

The next three days were fruitless for the *Graf Spee*, although on several occasions the order "General Quarters" was given, but the ships sighted proved to be useless to the raider's purpose and the tension was again relaxed.

On October 10, however, at six in the evening, the Harrison liner s.s. *Huntsman*, 8,000 tons, was proceeding on her lawful occasions under the command of Captain A. H. Brown of Rockferry, Cheshire. She had a crew of sixteen white men and sixty-seven Lascars.

Here was a plum worth plucking, for an 8,000-ton vessel whose considerable size would be reported by the *Graf Spee* look-outs might yield valuable oil and stores to replenish the raider's supplies.

The officer on the bridge of s.s. *Huntsman* informed Captain Brown that a man-of-war about five miles off the starboard bow was making for his ship.

The British skipper knew that there were French ships operating in the neighbourhood, but so did the *Graf Spee*. The *Dunkerque* was known to be in those waters.

As the battleship neared the *Huntsman*, Captain Brown was not surprised to see the French flag at her stern. He welcomed contact with an allied ship on what must have been a harassing voyage. He did not know that the German battleship *Graf Spee* was never averse to utilizing the flags of other nationals.

Captain Brown's astonishment changed to concern when he saw the French flag lowered and in its place the German swastika hoisted.

He immediately began to wireless for help, but hardly had the operator got a tap out of the instrument before the captain was ordered to quit and told that if he made any further attempt to use the wireless the *Huntsman* and her crew would be sunk immediately. So he could do nothing but stand by while Captain Langsdorff followed his familiar routine of despatching a boarding party from the *Graf Spee*.

When the boarding party had signalled their report a prize crew was sent aboard from the *Graf Spee* and Captain Brown, acting under orders, was told to follow the battleship.

At noon next day, however, she signalled

that she was off to find a neutral ship. The German captain's plan was to find a neutral whose master he would command to accept the crews of the *Newton Beech* and the *Huntsman* and to give them a passage home.

Captain Brown had his suspicions of this manœuvre as he was still acting under instructions from the German prize crew aboard his ship.

For three days the British ship was forced to steam in a north-westerly direction, but on the afternoon of the fourth, the *Graf Spee* did appear again and she had another ship in company with her.

But when the two approached, Captain Brown recognized the newcomer as a German cargo ship and not as the promised neutral vessel. No experienced seaman ever has much difficulty in recognizing a German vessel although in wartime they are ingeniously disguised. Their main outlines are characteristically German—square, squat and graceless.

A working party from the raider was sent aboard the *Huntsman*, which was immediately ordered to tie up alongside the newcomer.

The date was October 16, 1939, and the so-called neutral was, as Captain Brown had detected, a German Fleet Auxiliary, primarily used for supplying fuel, stores and ammunition.

Special ammunition lockers were a feature of her construction. She was oil-fuelled and her name *Altmark* was prominently displayed on her bows. The name meant nothing to Captain Brown, but he immediately saw that her derricks were swung out and her hatch covers were off—unmistakable signs that his fuel and stores were to be plundered.

The English master knew by the cut of her jib that the *Altmark* was one of the modern tankers, and in this he was right, for she had been built only eighteen months before.

He stood by helplessly and watched the transference of his stores and part of his cargo to the *Altmark*, and he and his officers and crew were then ordered to go aboard themselves. They were immediately joined by other prisoners from the *Graf Spee*. From the grimy decks of the Auxiliary ship they watched the refuelling of the raider, which then made off.

As soon as the *Altmark* got under way Captain Brown was taken to the commander of the German Auxiliary and the first moments of the interview left little doubt in his mind that the trip was to be no pleasure cruise.

He was faced by Captain J. S. Dau who, while treating him with tolerable civility, made him feel his position as prisoner. Captain Dau was short, thick-set and a trifle pompous. He was between sixty and seventy and what we should call in this country a "dug-out" who had been recalled to service at the outbreak of war.

He had served through the Great War and, according to his own statements, had been a prisoner in this country. Though he could never have been subjected to the conditions he imposed on his prisoners in the *Altmark* this fact seemed to have rankled in his mind.

There is no doubt that Dau was a good seaman or he would never have brought his ship through such trials and troubles as he did, crossing and recrossing the paths of the British patrols without detection, making and keeping assignations with the *Graf Spee* without casualty. But it was a pity he did not have more consideration for the unfortunate men who, through no fault of their own, and who were not belligerents, found themselves under his severe and sometimes tyrannical treatment.

He made it clear to Captain Brown that in any case the accommodation of the *Altmark* did not permit of special consideration being given to officers. He then turned to one of his officers and instructed him to take Captain Brown and his crew to their prison quarters.

On arriving on the 'tween deck Brown was shown into a dark, ill-lit space which proved to be an ammunition locker. His crew were taken down to similar accommodation on the lower deck.

Captain Brown saw at once that ventilation would be very inadequate and everywhere there was the inevitable reek and grime of oil. The men, he presumed, had to sleep on the steel plating of the deck, and he was given to understand that they would have to make their own sanitary arrangements.

The prisoners were soon to find that Dau was extreme in his punishments and the cell that was used as a detention-room was a disused tank in which a man could scarcely stand upright, and it had no sleeping or sanitary accommodation whatever.

On one occasion Captain Dau delivered himself of a tirade about Britain making war with Germany to enslave the German people, and said that his prisoners would be kept in confinement until Germany had the colonies to which she was justified. Although once he called all his captives aft and said that any requests from British prisoners white or black (this was to include the Lascars) would be turned down, he had his better moments. He made it clear that any cases of sickness among the prisoners would receive the same treatment as was given to his crew, and there is unanimous testimony to the generosity and humanity of the elderly doctor who strove to make conditions bearable for the British prisoners without being disloyal to his Captain.

Dau and his crew were often in difficulties themselves, particularly as regards water, as there was a fault in the condenser plant in the *Altmark*.

Dau was a tyrant but full recognition of the difficulties under which he worked in the ill-equipped *Altmark* must be made. The function of his ship as jackal to the *Graf Spee's* lion was exacting.

CHAPTER III

RAIDING AGAINST TIME

For several days the *Graf Spee* sought a further victim. Nearby the jackal *Altmark* skulked. Despite the raider's list of successes and her overwhelming strength there were grave misgivings on the part of Captain Langsdorff and of Captain Dau because the lion's kills had not been achieved without cost.

At her economic speed of 15 knots she had a 10,000-mile range but she had always to be prepared to speed up to 26 knots. This speed did not double her fuel consumption, it quadrupled it. Her settled policy was to "raid and run." She was not out to fight; neither was the *Altmark*, whose speed was similarly governed by conditions over which they had no control. Often both ships were compelled by the sight of an unidentified ship to steam several hundred miles out of their courses. Although the raider had planned meeting-places with supply ships, her Captain could never afford to cut deep into his reserves even when a day for a planned meeting was near at hand. Even within a few

54

hours of the arranged meeting for refuelling and re-storing he might have to cut and run with no chance of returning to the site for several days.

Several of his victims, from which he might legitimately expect to syphon oil, proved to be coal-burning and were of no use to him. Fuel was the raider's life-blood and maintenance of supply was a greater anxiety to the German captain than the possibility of meeting armed forces of the enemy. He could out-distance most of them with the start that was assured him by the range of vision from his tall control-tower. There is no natural cover at sea, but the raider had a great range of vision and roving aeroplanes to increase the distances. When fuel ran desperately low the Captain was facing his worst enemy.

But on October 22 the *Graf Spee* was in luck. She sighted a 5,000-ton vessel which proved to be s.s. *Trevanion*, Haim Shipping Co., New-castle-on-Tyne, whose master was Captain J. W. Edwards of Barry, South Wales.

The same ruthless procedure was carried out by the German raider, except that she derived immediate benefit from this kill, for substantial supplies of oil were syphoned from the tanker. Meantimes the Captain and his crew of fifty-three were transferred to the *Altmark* which was constantly in hovering attendance.

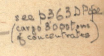

The surprise of the officers and men at finding British seamen already aboard was soon dissolved in an exchange of experiences and in forecasts of their hopes of release or possible internment if the raider eventually made for a home port.

It is probable that the *Graf Spee's* movements after she had sunk the *Trevanion* and had disappeared over the horizon were largely governed by her need for fuel. It is significant that the next ship she waylaid was the *Africa Shell*, which, although she had a gross tonnage of only 706, was potentially rich in oil. She belonged to the Anglo-Saxon Petroleum Company Limited, and was built as recently as February, 1939. She was divided into twelve tanks and had four centre tanks specially constructed for the carrying of case oil and for the carrying of oil in bulk.

When her Master, Captain F. G. Dove of Itham, Kent, sighted the *Graf Spee* on November 15, he was off Cape Sabora lighthouse, Portuguese East Africa. These were neutral waters and Captain Dove naturally felt that he was under the protection of international law. But the Nazi Germany has little respect for laws when it sees a chance of sinking British shipping.

The *Africa Shell* carried six European officers,

one Kenya officer and twenty-two native seamen.
She had no wireless.

Captain Dove was ordered by the *Graf Spee*
to leave the ship immediately with his crew.
Naturally he protested, but back came the
signal: "Clear off in ten minutes or we will sink
the ship!" There could be no sense in argument. After all, a 700-ton tanker was a speck
in the ocean beside a pocket battleship.

After such peremptory treatment Captain
Dove was surprised to find that its Commander,
Captain Hans Langsdorff, treated him with every
courtesy.

Indeed, on learning that Captain Dove had
lost his pipe overboard, the German Commander
sent him a new pipe, two pounds of tobacco and
some matches. Many a time Langsdorff invited
Captain Dove to his cabin for a chat, and left
the British skipper in no doubt that he was
sorry for the fate of the British merchant seamen, as they were not combatants, but civilians.
He remarked that in this war civilians, including
women and children, were involved just as much
as the fighting services. He told Captain Dove
that there was no reason why he should not
have as good a time as was possible during his
captivity and he was allowed almost complete
freedom in the German battleship. As a sailor
Langsdorff knew how Dove must feel as he saw

his ship sunk by the raider, and was man enough to apologize for his conduct. "It is the fortune of war," he said.

A very different atmosphere was radiated by Captain Dau of the *Altmark* when he frequently came aboard the *Graf Spee*. The two commanders, brought into closest co-operation by the dictates of war, were poles apart in their attitude to life and in their interpretation of the spirit of their duties. This was very evident when, on November 28, the Captain of the supply ship transferred British Captains, First and Second Engineers and Radio Officers to the *Graf Spee*.

Langsdorff seemed to prefer to have the "key" men under his own control, except in a few cases where the British masters were elderly. He also made it clear that he enjoyed their company. Dau's attitude was perhaps correct, but no more, towards his captives.

Thus far the raider had a record of grim, if not spectacular triumph. But her next victim was to sound her death-knell, though she can have had no knowledge of it, and the wireless operator of the *Doric Star* can scarcely have realized the vital importance of his signal because he was not able to pick up any acknowledgment of it.

The *Doric Star* was a much larger vessel; 550

feet in length and 10,000 gross tonnage. She was one of that fine type of ship known as a cargo liner, and she belonged to the Blue Star Line. In November she had picked up from New Zealand and Australia a cargo of 3,000 tons of frozen mutton and beef, 5,000 tons of butter and cheese and stocks of other commodities. She was a vital factor in the supply of Britain's food.

Her voyage had been uneventful until 1 p.m. on December 2, when Captain W. Stubbs heard a shot scream across his bows and saw a great column of water rise up where the projectile plunged into the sea not fifty yards away from his ship.

It was literally a bolt from the blue, because no ship had been reported to him and, indeed, no ship was in sight. This strange situation was accounted for by the lines of the *Graf Spee*. Like all other battleships she was very low-lying and the only superstructure that reared up at all was her control-tower. This was a very small target to spot and would probably not be discernible at all with the equipment available to the look-out of the *Doric Star*. But to the look-out in this control-tower, with every apparatus at his command, the considerable bulk of the *Doric Star* would be easily detected.

As the shell screamed across the bows of the

Doric Star her captain acted. Swiftly he called for the ship's position and instructed the Navigating Officer to tell the wireless operator to SOS:

"*S.* 20.10, *E.* 6.15, *gunned by battleship—Doric Star.*"

While the vital words were being transmitted Captain Stubbs gave the order to "heave-to" and bring her up into the weather. Firemen and trimmers came scrambling up from below, startled by the sudden stopping of the engines. Cooks peered through the galley ports and stewards paused in their duties.

Everyone on deck gazed expectantly at the black smudge that was rapidly taking shape in the quivering heat haze of the tropic summer morning. With startling suddenness, it seemed, the outlines of a battleship emerged from the mist. She was a formidable yet magnificent sight, but the feature that none missed was the for'ard turret with its huge guns.

The British skipper and his crew had no doubt about their fate. It was just a question of waiting to hear the sentence.

They had not long to wait. In the glittering sunlight the signalman on the signal platform of the battleship semaphored the message: "Do not transmit by wireless or I will immediately open fire!"

The buzz of the wireless died away. "Sparks" could only hope that his unceasing S O S had been picked up by someone who could make use of the information. The *Doric Star* had little hope of effective assistance, but if she had managed to convey the raider's proximity to the British Fleet her loss might not be entirely in vain.

Almost immediately came another visual message from the battleship. Captain Stubbs was ordered to take to the boats and to scuttle his ship. This is an order which every captain hopes he may never receive.

Faced with the inevitable the British skipper ordered the boats away and after satisfying himself that the crew was in the boats he and the ship's carpenter and mates saw that the water cocks were opened. Already the secret code book and Admiralty instructions had gone to the bottom in the weighted bag provided for this contingency.

The Captain of the German raider knew by her lines that the *Doric Star* was a meat-ship and, valuable as her heavy tonnage of meat and dairy produce might be as stores, they were useless to him because a pocket battleship has the smallest of refrigerators and no alternative facilities for storing such produce. Here indeed was a practical example of Germany's preference for guns rather than butter.

But the Germans were not satisfied to see the *Doric Star* slowly settling. If they could not take butter they were equally emphatic that no one else should take it. Time was pressing upon Captain Langsdorff and the slow sinking of the *Doric Star* might easily be impeded by a jammed cock. He gave himself no time to ascertain that the ship had been properly scuttled. He gave orders that the *Doric Star* should be sunk by shell-fire. Even that was not sufficient. His shortage of fuel was causing acute anxiety and his desire for further plunder may well have run things even too close for an audacious raider. He gave instructions that the battered meat-ship should be torpedoed. There could be no more striking indication of the nervous anxiety of Captain Langsdorff to be away. Time must indeed have been precious if he was ready to spend thousands of pounds on the speedier despatch of an already sinking ship. But the Chief Engineer had been insisting, with considerable vehemence, on the acute danger in which they would find themselves if they did not take immediate steps to refuel.

The *Graf Spee* had been as far east as Madagascar in the Indian Ocean and then, rounding

The explosion as the British steamer "Ashlea" was blown up by a torpedo from the "Graf Spee."

the Cape of Good Hope (well to the southward as there is a British Naval Dockyard at Simonstown), had been active in the vast waters of the Atlantic trade routes.

So as soon as they got the Master and chief officers of the *Doric Star* aboard, and his crew of sixty-four aboard the *Altmark*, the pocket battleship turned south and made for her rendezvous with her supply ship, *Ussukuma*.

The raider called upon several supply ships, only one of which, the *Altmark*, was used as a prison ship. The routine with raiding ships is to arrange their rendezvous weeks beforehand, off the trade routes. In the days of coal fuel it was necessary to use deserted islands or unfrequented inlets, but to-day, with oil fuel, given reasonably fine weather, the operation can be carried out anywhere at sea.

The *Ussukuma*, under a neutral flag, would fill her own tanks at some port where detection was unlikely and ready cash was appreciated. If the raider had found it necessary to alter the original date or meeting place, the supply ship would be informed at the port and would adjust her movements accordingly.

Most of the time of the supply ships was occupied in loitering at a low speed and avoiding any chance of challenge until the appointed day arrived. Their captains were invariably

Naval Reserve Officers who knew the routine of raiding and could be relied upon to keep the vital appointments if it were humanly possible.

But like many a successful hunter, the German raider could not resist what appeared to be an easy "kill," even on the way to a rendezvous. The *Graf Spee* had done only a few hours' steaming when, on the morning of December 3, one of her reconnaissance planes, catapulted from her deck, brought news of the sighting of the *Tairoa*, about 150 miles south of the *Doric Star's* position and steering NNW.

She was a fine cargo steamer of 8,000 tons owned by Furness, Withy & Co., Ltd., and under the command of Captain W. B. S. Starr of Liverpool.

"I was unaware that I had been sighted by the scouting aeroplane," said Captain Starr, "and I thought the course I was steering would take me sufficiently far to the westward of *Doric Star's* position for safety if the attacking vessel was a submarine. Nevertheless, I was feeling very uneasy about my position because, of course, I didn't know the nature of the raider. She might have been an armed merchant cruiser, a submarine or a pocket battleship. I left orders for a call at 4 a.m. on December 3.

"I arrived on the bridge shortly after 4 a.m.

and half an hour later, with the first streak of dawn in the sky, a faint smudge appeared on the port bow. It was the *Graf Spee* and she had calculated our course and speed all too well, and was waiting to make her next 'kill.'

"I gave orders at once to call all hands and clear away the boats, but as there was still a hope that the approaching vessel might be one of our own cruisers, and not the enemy, I waited to make sure before sending out an S O S call.

"The battleship closed in on us very quickly flying the French flag, but when about two miles distant she ran up the German ensign, gave us the signal: 'Stop your engines,' and fired a shot across our bows.

"I then told Mr. P. J. Cummins, the wireless operator, to send out the following signal:

"'*Lat.* 21° 38'.5. *Long.* 3° 13' *W. Attacked by German Battleship Admiral Scheer.*'

"A bad guess on my part!

"This signal Mr. Cummins sent out two and a half times, and only stopped doing so when the instrument was destroyed. [For this brave act he was subsequently awarded the M.B.E.]

"Immediately the wireless started the *Graf Spee* opened fire on us, shells bursting on the bridge, Captain's cabin, officers' quarters and wireless-room. One wing of the bridge was wrecked, the steering gear put out of action, and the port boats badly damaged with flying shrapnel.

"As soon as the wireless instrument was destroyed the firing ceased. Five men were wounded; three, Leedale, Farmer and Dixon, all deck boys, rather badly. That the casualties were so low we have to thank Providence and the humanity of the Captain of the *Graf Spee*, who used only his smallest guns to achieve his purpose.

"Meanwhile I had given orders to get the boats away and two of the starboard boats were lowered and manned with most of the crew. I had planned to make for St. Helena, about five hundred miles NW. of our position. However, just as we were going to push off, the boarding party from the *Graf Spee* came alongside in their launch and ordered everyone back on board.

"They then searched the ship for confidential papers, but in that they were disappointed as there had been plenty of time to put them over the side.

"Having searched the ship and cleared out the store-rooms, all my crew were taken to the *Graf Spee*, and at about 7.30 a.m. the *Tairoa* was sunk by gunfire, the secondary armament being used for this purpose.

"Captain Langsdorff of the *Graf Spee* sent for

me immediately on my arrival on board and apologized for having to fire on a merchant ship, but excused himself for doing so on the plea that I had failed to obey his signal to stop my wireless. I am afraid in the excitement of the encounter I had not seen the signal.

"Captain Langsdorff seemed very concerned about my wounded men and personally visited them on more than one occasion. He also sent for Mr. Cummins and congratulated him on his bravery in continuing to send out his message until the instrument was shot away.

"The *Graf Spee* was disguised as the *Deutschland* on the day she captured us, having a dummy funnel, made of canvas, abaft the real funnel, and a dummy superimposed turret forward. These were taken down before we left the *Graf Spee* three days later.

"No time was lost in getting away from the vicinity of the *Tairoa's* sinking, a SW. course being taken, and three days later the *Altmark* was sighted and the crews of the *Doric Star* and *Tairoa* transferred to her. That night, December 6, the *Graf Spee* filled up with fuel oil from the *Altmark*, and we did not see or hear of her again until nearly two and a half months later.

"Before leaving the *Graf Spee* I had a long talk with Captain Langsdorff in his cabin. He impressed me as a man of great humanity, with a distaste for his job of raiding unarmed vessels, and a healthy respect for the British Navy."

There was little enthusiasm among Captain Langsdorff's engineers for this delay over the *Tairoa*. The further kill had done nothing to relieve their difficulties. The rendezvous for re-fuelling was an isolated spot well off the trade routes in Longitude 40 W., Latitude 30 S. There were still about 1,500 miles to cover, and her Captain took the risk of cutting even deeper into his scanty fuel reserves by increasing speed to 20 knots. Such risks had to be taken in war. He had almost completed a thousand of his 1,500 miles when, on the afternoon of December 7, just after eight bells, his look-out reported a ship dead ahead.

If there was one victim of the *Graf Spee* that was not taken by surprise, or at least not taken unprepared, it was this ship, the steamer *Streon-shalh*. She was a vessel of nearly 4,000 tons, and had as her master Captain J. J. Robinson of Runswick Bay, York, who in his twenty-five years of life at sea had been torpedoed in s.s. *Kildare* in 1917, and again in s.s. *Ingleside* in the following year. The *Streonshalh*, owned by Headlam & Son of Whitby, carried nearly 6,000 tons of wheat, shipped from Rosario and consigned to the Ministry of Food. She left

Montevideo with a crew of thirty-two all told on November 28, "in good condition and well found." The ship was not in convoy and the Master carried out boat-drill and fire-drill regularly every fortnight. Life-boats were kept swung out all the time.

Captain Robinson set and carried out the instructed course until 4.10 p.m. on December 7. At that hour his Chief Officer, Mr. T. W. Mallinson, reported a vessel on the horizon which proved to be the *Graf Spee* approaching from the SSE.

As the *Graf Spee* closed with her, Captain Langsdorff was surprised to see great activity on board. Boats were being lowered and crew and stores were being got on board as swiftly as possible. One thing was evident to the raider; the food-ship was British, for from the main mast flew the Red Duster of Britain's Mercantile Marine. Captain Robinson in this case only used it as a gesture of spirited defiance, which those who knew Langsdorff's character have little doubt would have been respected.

Subsequent events cannot be more concisely presented than in the sworn statement of the British Master.

The German raider "came close to and signalled by flag: 'Do not transmit by wireless or I will immediately open fire.'

"It was not known that the ship was a German warship until she was close up, as the flag could not be seen. I stopped my ship after seeing the German flag, and instructed the first and third officers to lower the port and starboard life-boats and to take the bulk of the crew away from the ship. My chief engineer (Mr. F. Jefferies), second officer, bo'sun, one A.B. and myself remained on ship. A boarding party, twenty-five men armed, came on board. The officer in charge told me that my ship would be sunk. He enquired for secret papers and code book, but I had already thrown these overboard in a heavily weighted bag. The ship was searched. Meanwhile one of *Streonshalh's* boat crews was recalled on board and the chief officer's boat proceeded to the *Graf Spee*.

"Each hatch was opened and one bomb put in each hold, four altogether. All the British crew were then ordered into the launch of *Graf Spee*, and taken on board that ship, and put down below. After that I saw nothing, but about 5.30 p.m. the bombs were heard exploding, and gunfire was also heard.

"Later on a German officer stated that the *Streonshalh* had sunk, but that bombs had not been sufficient to sink her and that she sank by the head."

70

These fresh captives found that they were fairly treated on board the German pocket battleship and the Commander's conduct to them was correct in every way. They had no cause for complaint and if occasionally they were critical of the food they knew that it was no worse than that served to the ship's German crew at the same time. Raiding over a vast area, when the chief consideration is victims, inevitably produces discomforts due to depleted stores.

Captain Langsdorff called it a day, and sat down to examine the results of his raiding. He felt satisfied by results but was seriously inconvenienced not only by depleted fuel but by depleted stores. He had too many captives to house and feed. Something must be done to get the *Graf Spee* back to her normal complement. This is where the jackal could come in.

The *Altmark* was signalled to contact him, and her Captain received instructions to take further captives on board.

No doubt Captain Langsdorff would have been glad to have been relieved of all his prisoners, although possibly his inherent decency suggested that captains and chief engineers should be allowed to remain in the better accommodation of his own ship. He knew the congestion which already existed in the unsatisfactory accommodation in the tanker *Altmark*.

cee p 69 — 7th December

THE BATTLE OF THE PLATE

The German Commander retained five captains, seven officers and fifty-one members of the crews. At the same time Captain Langsdorff recalled his prize crews from the *Newton Beech* and *Huntsman*, transferred their remaining personnel to the already overcrowded *Altmark* and sank the two British ships by shell-fire.

The lion was no longer interested in the jackal. She was instructed to return to Germany with her prisoners. Meantime the *Graf Spee* sped on to her rendezvous. All that was needed now was a pause for refuelling and revictualling and the lion could set out again in her strength.

was sunk 7 Oct

was sunk 17 Oct?

72

CHAPTER IV

RENDEZVOUS

CAPTAIN LANGSDORFF felt very satisfied. His sinking of the *Doric Star* on Saturday, December 2, with the loss of thousands of tons of British food, had rounded off a productive week. His satisfaction would have been gravely undermined had he known the facts of a subsequent sinking two thousand miles away.

Almost due west, off the coast of Brazil, H.M.S. *Ajax*, in the course of her patrol, sighted a strange ship. The British cruiser was the flagship of the South American Squadron and entitled to fly the broad pennant of Commodore H. H. Harwood, who was aboard. The Commander of the *Ajax* was Captain C. H. L. Woodhouse.

To the lower deck these brilliant officers were known as "Flip" Harwood and "One-a-day-Wimpy." There could be no more sincere tribute to the esteem in which they were held than the bestowal of these nick-names. The origin of "Flip" is obscure, but the history of "One-a-day Wimpy" is in no doubt. Indeed,

73

it arose from circumstances that are the more thrilling because they have not yet been revealed.

It is not in Britain's interests to announce all her successes in the sinking of German shipping, but Captain Woodhouse's record of "kills" was so remarkable and consistent that his habit of sinking a German ship a day became something like a tradition—hence the name.

But on the morning of Sunday, December 2, after "Divisions," the shrill pipe of the bo'sun was heard and the shout, "Clear lower deck. Everybody aft!" was transmitted through the loud-speakers to all parts of the ship.

Immediately the crew came tumbling up from below, stokers and cooks—in fact everyone but the skeleton guns' crews and the watch-keepers.

The excitement in the jostling crowd could not be hidden. Something important was moving, and it was soon seen that the Commodore himself was to address the men.

Commodore Harwood with his instinct for leadership immediately took the crew into his confidence. He told them that he had received information that the "ghost ship" had been located. She had sunk a Blue Star vessel, the *Doric Star*, on the previous day. He further intimated that he was also aware of the fact that a supply ship was sailing south, presumably for a rendezvous with the raider who must by now be very short of oil and provisions. He was going north to search for this ship and he wanted the strictest vigilance and watchfulness from everybody.

This news was a grand tonic. The men's spirits swiftly reacted to this possibility of coming to grips with the raider herself, and they responded with zest to the confidence placed in them.

They had but two days to wait. On the evening of December 5 they sighted a strange ship off the port bow. The crew's excitement was momentarily diminished because, as *Ajax* closed with the strange ship, there was some doubt as to whether she was the supply ship in question, or even another enemy craft to be added to the cruiser's "kills."

She was sailing under a neutral ensign, an 8,000-ton ship with the white upper-works of a passenger liner, though from the derricks in her well-decks she must also carry substantial cargo. *Ajax* signalled to her to stop her engines. The stranger hove-to. There was immediate activity in the British cruiser. A whaler, hanging from the falls, was quickly lowered to the water's edge. The officer in the stern sheets saw to his revolver. Too often heavily armed enemy ships were disguised as innocent neutrals.

The boarding party had their rifles to hand and the clips were filled.

As the whaler approached the steamer's side the officer called "Bow." The man in the bow shipped his oar and picked up the boat-hook ready to hook on.

"Way enough."

The men ceased rowing.

"Oars."

With easy precision the crew shipped their oars.

A man leaned over the side of the merchant-man and dropped a Jacob's ladder. By this time the bowman had hooked on to the rope which had been paid out. The officer in charge of the boarding party, awaiting his opportunity, grasped the ladder and shinned up the ship's side. He swung himself over the bulwarks with his men close behind him.

Turning to the petty officer he said: "Stand the party at the 'ready.' I'm going to interview the skipper."

"Ay, ay, sir"—and the rifle butts struck the deck.

The officer in charge sprang up the companion-way to the bridge.

He was not satisfied with the ship's papers and ordered that the Captain and officers should

Keystone

THE "ALTMARK" (at left) DURING HEIGHT OF HER CAREER. PHOTO-
GRAPH TAKEN FROM THE DECK OF THE "GRAF SPEE" AS THE CREW
FROM THE CAPTURED BRITISH FREIGHTER "HUNTSMAN" WAS TRANS-
FERRED TO THE "ALTMARK."

Planet

THE BLOWING UP OF THE "DORIC STAR" BY A TORPEDO FROM THE
"GRAF SPEE," TWO OF WHOSE GUNS ARE SEEN IN THE FOREGROUND.

be placed under open arrest, thus relieving them of their authority while the British conducted the search.

He then called upon the crew to open up the hatches and proceeded to make the most thorough inspection. So far he had found nothing incriminating, but his suspicions had not been dissolved.

Cases were now being brought on deck and opened at his direction. Most of the stores revealed were quite innocuous, but to his satisfaction some of the cases were found to contain intricate machine parts which were certainly unexpected in such surroundings. Further examination of them revealed that they were probably intended for a big fighting unit. It was a reasonable assumption that they were now on board the masquerading supply vessel of the ghost ship which the *Ajax* had been hunting so assiduously. Expert scrutiny tended to confirm these assumptions, and to suggest that these complicated parts were made for a pocket battleship.

Armed with this information the officer signalled to Captain Woodhouse in the *Ajax* that the suspicious merchantman was probably a supply ship for the German raider.

Captain Woodhouse gave immediate instructions for the crew of the merchantman to be transferred to the *Ajax*, and after a further search to ensure that no living creature was left aboard the supply ship, the balance of the boarding party returned to the *Ajax*, which then sank the merchantman by shell-fire.

This fresh influx of prisoners put the *Ajax* in similar difficulties to those experienced by the *Graf Spee*. The Commodore instructed H.M.S. *Cumberland* to close with her and transferred 107 prisoners to that ship for passage to the Falklands.

The German prisoners left H.M.S. *Ajax* with regret because they were on excellent terms with their captors. On one occasion their spokesman asked if they might be allowed to relieve the monotony of their captivity by joining up with the ship's working parties. Captain Woodhouse had no objection to this reasonable request, and instructed the First Lieutenant to arrange working parties among the prisoners who for several days shared the labours of the British crew in keeping *Ajax* efficient and clean.

Ajax was now well set for the big "kill." She had refuelled, watered and given shore leave at the Falklands a week before. Finding no mail at Port Stanley the Commodore instructed H.M.S. *Achilles* to repair to Montevideo to pick it up and made a rendezvous with her for December 11.

The next morning *Ajax* sighted another cargo liner. At first sight she had a strange superficial resemblance to the *Ussukuma*. Her white upper-works and short, squat funnel were noticeably similar. She was flying the French flag, but nevertheless *Ajax* signalled her to stop and sent a boarding party to examine her. In a very short while the boarding officer signalled that she was, indeed, a French vessel; the *Formose*, bound for Buenos Aires, there to load a cargo of frozen meat.

The British cruiser escorted the French merchantman to port, and it is not unlikely that the continued association with the ship underlined in the British officers' minds the similarity between the presumed supply ship of the raider, which they had previously sunk, and the French *Formose*.

On Sunday, December 10, the shrill pipe of the bos'n again sounded after "Divisions." There was keen expectation of the Commodore's next announcement. This was, indeed, a game in which every man felt he was a vital factor.

Commodore Harwood now revealed his plans in sharp detail. With his Commander and officers he had calculated the rendezvous which the raider had presumably arranged with the supply ship *Ussukuma*. It was possible that the raider was a pocket battleship, and as such a doughty opponent. He outlined to the men the raider's superior armaments, which would outrange them by more than two miles, and added that he had ordered *Achilles* and *Exeter* to join up with *Ajax* with the utmost despatch. He told them that he was meeting *Achilles* the next morning, with home mails aboard, and that *Exeter*, then in the north, was hastening to meet them.

So confident was the Commodore of the calculations that he told the men they could look for the raider in the early hours of December 13, either dead ahead or a little to the starboard. He even went so far as to offer a pound to the first man who spotted her.

With such revealed trust in their confidence the men responded wholeheartedly to the Commodore's order for the utmost vigilance and watchfulness every moment of the day and night.

After the excitement of the home mail from *Achilles*, the tension was resumed next day by the appearance of H.M.S. *Exeter*, with her two tall slender masts first showing above the northern horizon.

The South American Division was at full strength and waiting for the battle-call. But Great Britain has a staunch Ally in this war and it was her privilege to assist in an unspectacular but vital way.

It had been arranged that the Master of the French merchantman, *Formose*, should play a dangerous role, and his ready compliance and co-operation deserve the highest commendation. His ship was to take the place of the now non-existent *Ussukuma*, and keep a daring rendezvous with the German ghost ship. The French Master had no doubt about the strategy of the British captains, nor of the effectiveness of their help, but there were other factors in his engagement over which the British Navy could have no control.

He was to sail out into the estuary of the Plate, ostensibly as the *Ussukuma*, in the early hours of December 13.

At the appointed hour the fast British cruisers would be approaching from the south, keeping well below the skyline until the enemy raider had swallowed the bait, or at least ventured sufficiently far into the trap to make escape a most hazardous undertaking.

If the raider came from the north-east and sighted no supply ship the instant doubts in the mind of her Captain would probably result in the reversal of his plans before the British ships, approaching from the south, could hope to make effective contact or to pursue her profitably if she retreated.

The *Formose*, by this daring plan, would have

to face hours of acute suspense and risk complete destruction at any moment. No one could forecast the instant of revelation. The German raider might, immediately she came within sight of the French merchantman, detect the ruse and sink her forthwith.

Alternatively, desperately anxious for the rendezvous and duped by the resemblance of the two ships, he might come within a few miles without any suspicion being aroused. But with Gallic logic the French Master knew that inevitably recognition could not be long delayed. Even if the raider were drawn close enough to her supposed supply ship to allow the British cruisers to reveal themselves, the first reaction of a commander, the more so if he suddenly saw formidable opposition, would probably be to sink the ship that had tricked him before turning his attention to the enemy.

With the plans carefully laid, on the night of Tuesday, December 12, H.M.S. *Ajax*, *Achilles* and *Exeter* steamed north off the Patagonian coast; in company and each about twelve miles apart.

The atmosphere on board the British cruisers was tense. There is no relaxation, day or night, when cruisers are patrolling. Now, with the knowledge of an approaching action, the very ships themselves seemed to be spoiling for a fight.

Before the soft darkness of the sub-tropic night had descended armourers had touched up gun fittings, ammunition hoists were oiled and tried out, magazines opened up, bags of cordite laid alongside shells. Fire hoses were bent on cocks and everywhere was an atmosphere of tension; the tension that comes not from anxiety but from confident strength and preparedness. The dazzling stars were reflected in the phosphorescent sea, but there were no lights of any kind upon the British cruisers. It was more than a man's life was worth even to smoke on deck, for the glow of the cigarette might betray his ship's position, and a torpedo might not only destroy the ship but frustrate the plan upon which so much depended.

Meantime there was mysterious activity aboard the French merchantman, *Formose*. Few members of the ship's company shared the Captain's secret, and as a result there were many comments upon his seemingly rash departure from the safety of neutral waters without escort. There was no lack of shipping in Buenos Aires to point the dangers. The crews of many ships then loading testified to the activities of the raider who was harassing the trade routes. But the French captain seemed to have an almost fatalistic confidence in his movements. He steamed ahead into the darkness with magnificent assurance and resolution.

Yet even his unshakable calm could not quite reassure his crew. They obeyed without questioning, but their perplexity was apparent. They knew nothing of the approaching British cruisers, and no whisper had come to their ears that they were about to offer themselves as a bait to the mighty raider.

The French master had no doubt that if he had informed his crew they would enter into the adventure with zest, but espionage was so rife in the South American ports and the German population so preponderant that the merest whisper of this daring ruse might have endangered not only the *Formose* but the whole strategy which had been built up with her co-operation.

In the darkness of their ignorance and of the night they sped on.

At that very moment the *Graf Spee* was approaching from the north-east. Her engineers had daily reiterated the urgent need for refuelling, but now they were within sight of salvation. In a few hours the *Ussukuma* would be sighted. The lion, refreshed, would stalk abroad undaunted.

In the soft darkness Fate held her breath.

It was midnight on December 12.

CHAPTER V

THE FIGHT IS ON

The sun was rising over the eastern sea as the French cargo liner steamed slowly into the South Atlantic. She was unarmed and without escort. Despite the many true and untrue stories that had been rife in Buenos Aires concerning an armed raider that was harassing those waters, sinking ships and taking the crews prisoners, she ventured out alone. Yet, as he stood on the bridge that early morning and peered through the golden haze, her Captain seemed quite unaware of any danger.

Suddenly the drowsiness of the morning was broken by the clang of a bell. The look-out on the fo'c'sle-head had spotted a smudge of smoke away on the port bow, and with two strokes of the bell had signalled this fact to the bridge.

With no trace of excitement the Frenchman turned and gazed through his binoculars at the shapeless smoke. He watched intently for some minutes. Whatever ship it was she was speedy, for she was quickly coming into view.

He rapped out an order to the quarter master:

"Engines half-speed ahead!"

"Engines half-speed ahead!" repeated the quartermaster, and the handle of the engine-room telegraph swung round and finished at that signal.

The ship began to lose speed. The smudge of smoke took definite shape and soon it was clear that the approaching ship was no ordinary merchantman. She had a familiar superstructure forward of a short, squat funnel and was painted a dull grey which made her outlines merge with the sea and smoke. As the two ships converged the stranger's foredeck became clearly discernible, and from her for'ard turret could gradually be distinguished three long, vicious-looking guns.

The French captain nodded to himself.

Clearly this was a marauder for which he was acting as bait—a fine prize, if she could be induced to walk into the carefully prepared trap.

The *Formose's* Master swept the horizon with his glasses. There was a grim smile on his face as he did so. There was no sign of the promised assistance, but his faith remained unshaken. He waited, expecting at any moment to receive an order from the raider to "Heave-to!" But he might not be given that courtesy; he might receive a shot across his bows, or even amidships, if the raider had already detected what was afoot.

He looked again to the south, and this time discerned a faint smudge of smoke. To another's eye it might have been only a variation of the morning mist, but to him it was of far greater significance. He had no fear of the British Navy's failing him. But would they, could they, come in time? That depended now upon the raider and how long he himself could maintain the pretence.

So far the enemy warship was approaching as though she had no suspicions. There was no order to "Heave-to!" and no warning shot. But it might be only a matter of moments. That the raider did not stand on ceremony he knew from skippers in Buenos Aires.

Then suddenly events took a fresh turn.

The battleship, which had been approaching at high speed, and with such apparent confidence, changed her course and headed almost due east. Presumably she had sighted the smudge of smoke to the southward. To the raider, several miles to the north of the *Formose*, it could have revealed little detail, but what it revealed was apparently enough.

The raider, without making a signal or firing

a shot, turned to leave the French decoy and to engage the newcomer.

The *Formose* had played her part excellently. Now all that remained for her was to get clear of the battle zone.

"Port engine full ahead, starboard engine full astern!" her Master ordered, and the quartermaster jumped to the engine-room telegraph and rang down to the engines.

"Helm hard over," yelled the Captain, and the man at the wheel swung round the spokes in obedience to the order. The French ship shuddered at the sudden strain and slowly began to turn.

Once her bow was pointed to the westward and to the safety of neutral shipping, her skipper rang down:

"Full speed ahead, both engines!"

She was soon showing her stern to the battleship from the north and to the British cruiser from the south, but the *Formose* had done her courageous part. She had duped the German raider whose Captain, harassed by the urgent demands of his engineers, had picked out the details of his apparent supply ship with intense relief.

Captain Langsdorff felt more satisfied than he had done for some days. At last he was within an ace of satisfying the imperative demands of his engineers. He was within a few miles of salvation. Already he could discern the hull of the supply ship which, as he had never doubted, was there to keep the rendezvous.

Orders had previously been passed to the engine-room staff to shackle on the oil cocks and to stand by for refuelling. Store-rooms had been swept out, working parties were ready, but meantime everything was in full battle order because the raider could not count on immunity from attack, even though she calculated that her rendezvous was safe.

The raider was now close enough to see the white upper-works of the supply ship. They were conspicuous in the morning sun. She was a satisfying sight, to captain and crew, for the raider had been on short commons.

Suddenly the look-out signalled: "Ship on the port beam!"

Swiftly the German commander swept his binoculars round to the south. It was a moment of suspense, for from the look-out on the high control-tower which the Captain had ascended to pick up the supply ship, he spotted the unmistakable tall, slim masts of H.M.S. *Exeter*.

His first thoughts were for the protection of his supply ship. He turned his glasses on her again. She must have seen the oncoming British ship before his glasses had found her. Why had she not flashed a signal to him?

As he watched her intently, all his doubts were dissolved. She swiftly began to turn. She gave no message. Perhaps she had decided to run for the safety of neutral waters. But as she turned and presented a broadside view to the German captain, he saw in a flash that this was not the supply ship, *Ussukuma*, but a similar merchantman that had apparently been used as a decoy.

He was trapped.

The Captain was a fighter, but as Commander of a raider his instructed policy was to "Raid and run, raid and run. . . ." His maximum usefulness to his country was to harass the trade routes and sink enemy merchantmen, and not to risk being sunk or even disabled. His very presence in the waters was sufficient to hold up heavy tonnage of allied shipping and to embarrass home supplies.

"Raid and run . . . raid and run. . . ."

He rapped out the orders to put the ship about and rang down to the engine-room: "Full speed ahead both engines!"

Now, after the numbness of discovery, feeling returned. His first reaction was to despatch the ship that had duped him, but wiser thoughts prevailed.

Immediately the buzz of alarms sounded all over the ship.

"Action Stations!" There was no mistaking the urgency of the noise; it produced a tattoo of hastening steps all over the ship. It brought consternation to the crew. They had been used to jumping to "General Quarters," for this was the evolution whenever a strange ship was sighted. But "Action Stations" was outside their experience. Indeed on several occasions Captain Langsdorff had assured his very young crew that they would never have to fight. They were serving a raider, and a raider whose speed was sufficient to show a clean pair of heels to any opposition.

So far their Captain's promise had been fulfilled. They had never been in any danger; never even been challenged.

The news ran round the ship like fire: "It's a British man-of-war!" This was the raider's first challenge, but they never expected their Captain to accept it. The enemy was only just within sight. That gave them a fourteen-mile start. It would be more than sufficient. They stood to their stations with confidence, having implicit faith in their commander and his ship. Even so there was a tenseness about the atmosphere that alarmed the crew. They could see the main magazines being opened up, the hoists being tried out. The sight of the stretcher parties hurrying to their stations was unnerving. Hitherto the closest they had been to action was when the raider used her smaller armaments for sinking a victim. Now she was at least cleared for action as a precaution, but the miles of sea between her and the still scarcely visible British cruiser were some reassurance.

To the British prisoners in the marauder, mostly merchant skippers and key men from the ships which the raider had sunk, the buzz of alarm brought consternation and perplexity.

They had become used to the sounds on board when an unarmed vessel was sighted. The formula was depressingly familiar. They heard the " General Quarters," engines stopped, boat lowered and the boarding party called away. These sounds were too familiar to be comfortable. Now they listened helplessly, for they were indeed victims of an identical procedure. Every time "General Quarters" went they relived the scene in which their own particular ships had been sunk. There was gloomy speculation among them as to the identity of the latest victim. Whenever fresh prisoners were brought aboard, there was the chance of seeing old shipmates compelled to share their imprisonment. The only consolation was that sometimes

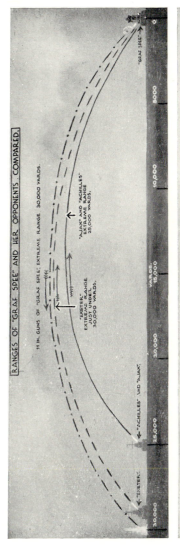

RANGES OF "GRAF SPEE" AND HER OPPONENTS COMPARED.

11 IN. GUNS OF "GRAF SPEE" EXTREME RANGE 30,000 YARDS.

"AJAX" AND "ACHILLES"
EXTREME RANGE
25,000 YARDS.

"EXETER"
EXTREME RANGE
JUST UNDER
30,000 YARDS.

"GRAF SPEE"

"ACHILLES" AND "AJAX".

"EXETER".

YARDS.

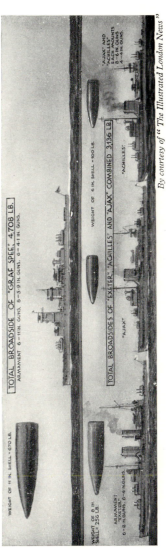

WEIGHT OF 11 IN. SHELL 670 LB.

TOTAL BROADSIDE OF "GRAF SPEE," 4,708 LB.
ARMAMENT 6—11 IN. GUNS, 8—5·9 IN. GUNS, 6—4·1 IN. GUNS.

WEIGHT OF 6 IN. SHELL 100 LB.

"AJAX" AND
"ACHILLES"
EACH MOUNTS
8—6 IN. GUNS
4—4 IN. GUNS

"ACHILLES"

"AJAX"

TOTAL BROADSIDES OF "EXETER," "ACHILLES" AND "AJAX" COMBINED 3,136 LB.

WEIGHT OF 8 IN
SHELL 256 LB.

ARMAMENT
6—8 IN. GUNS, 6—4 IN. GUNS.
"EXETER."

By courtesy of " The Illustrated London News "

the fresh influx of captives brought later news.

But clearly now there was some abnormal alarm; such activities as sounded overhead were not caused merely by the sighting of another potential victim.

The iron doors of the quarters in which some of the British prisoners were housed were suddenly clanged to with violence. Three long blasts sounded on the siren. An officer of the raider ran to another group of British prisoners who were tumbling out of their hammocks and said: "Gentlemen, I'm afraid we must leave you to your own devices to-day." Before they had time to question him the door was locked on the outside.

Apprehensions chased across the minds of the prisoners like clouds across the summer sky. They consulted swiftly and as the ceaseless tattoo of running feet sounded over their heads they were not unduly disturbed. They knew the Captain's policy was "Raid and run," and they knew also that he had no doubts as to his ability to elude any challenge. Apparently now he was preparing for action, but Captain Langsdorff's repeated assurances, coupled with their own observations, convinced them that they were not in much danger. They did not imagine that the British Navy had any

93

comparable ship in those waters. The German captain was well informed of the disposition of the British ships. He knew that the South American Squadron was in those waters, he knew that *Exeter* and *Ajax* had been joined by *Achilles* at the outbreak of war. But the vast waters of the South Atlantic still gave him plenty of scope. He had made several rendezvous and kept them without interruption. But now the British Navy had found him out. All thoughts of the supply ship vanished. His one anxiety was to get to sea. He had every confidence that escape would be successful. He did not fear his speed against that of the *Exeter*, and he had a good start. A stern chase was always a long one, and if he could gain cover of night before the British ship got dangerously near, he might easily evade her.

True, she might send out her 'plane next morning to discover him, but the machine was not a bomber and his anti-aircraft guns could dispose of it. If it evaded them the 'plane could do comparatively little damage to the raider.

He would cut and run.

The engine-room telegraph rang "Ahead" on one engine, "Astern" on the other. He put the helm hard over and the warship quivered at the sudden strain.

The crew, standing to their posts, watched the evolution with gladness. Their Captain was as good as his word. He was not going to face the enemy and subject them to the terrible ordeal of a sea battle. Soon the "Carry on!" would be given and they would be back at their ordinary tasks.

But below, in the engine-room, astonishment was quickly followed by consternation. "Full speed ahead on both engines" had now been signalled on the telegraph. And the ship was steering almost due east. That meant she was making for the trackless area of the South Atlantic.

Only the previous evening the engineer had informed the Captain, in the privacy of his cabin, that the ship was woefully short of fuel. Langsdorff had replied that he was meeting a supply ship at daybreak and they would then refuel to capacity and resume their role of raider.

The engineer thought they were running things very close, but the Captain reassured him. Certainly the Captain's record justified his confidence. They had never been in difficulties yet.

But now the ship was heading for the open sea with a very low reserve of fuel. It was suicidal, and the engineer made his way to the bridge to tell Captain Langsdorff the plain truth of the case.

From the argument one fact emerged. Escape was impossible. The alternative was inescapable. They must fight. A fight was contrary to the raider's plans, but her Commander faced the outcome with confidence.

He was well aware that ship for ship he had every advantage. His main armament was far heavier and therefore of greater range and accuracy. All guns lose in accuracy as the range increases but light more than heavy ones. Heavier projectiles retain their velocity longer and they do not "spread" so much, so on all counts the raider could easily dispose of the *Exeter*.

His plan therefore was to turn and make for the estuary of the Plate, disposing of the enemy in his passage.

The two ships were now about fourteen miles apart, and although the hull of the *Exeter* could not be seen from the deck of the raider yet she was visible to the officers and men in the control-tower.

Meanwhile the look-outs aboard *Exeter* had reported a ship off the starboard bow. Captain F. S. Bell took a look through his binoculars. Yes, there was the vindication of their strategy, confirmation of their calculations; this was indeed the "ghost ship" and without doubt she was a pocket battleship, as they had surmised.

The British cruiser was long since cleared for action; her crew were at Action Stations. Captain Bell had watched with satisfaction the French merchantman steaming innocently on her apparently foolhardy voyage. She was still in danger but she had fulfilled her part magnificently. It was now up to the Navy.

From the bridge Captain Bell had watched the raider emerge from the early morning haze, watched her speeding with almost arrogant confidence towards the supposed supply ship and then almost instantly had seen her make a double turn; first out to sea and then as quickly towards the land.

There could only be one reason for this extraordinary manœuvre. She must be running short of fuel. As the raider turned towards the estuary the *Exeter* also altered course and the two ships were running parallel at about fourteen miles apart.

The raider swung her fore and aft turrets to port, placed her guns at the requisite elevation and fired a salvo at her foe. A blinding flash, a belch of smoke and over four thousand pounds of steel and high explosives were sent screaming in the direction of the *Exeter*. But before the whine of the shells was heard on that ship she had accepted the challenge.

The fight was on.

When the raider fired her first broadside all her guns were directed on one object—the *Exeter*, but the shells did not all drop in the same place; some were ahead and some beyond the target; some to the right, some to the left. This is called the "spread" and by its means accurate range was established. If all the splashes from a first salvo are seen by the spotting officer to fall short, the next is fired say 500 yards beyond. If the shells are still falling short another 500 yards is added. If now all the splashes are seen to fall over the ship the range is dropped until some shells fall over and some short. This is known as "straddling."

The main armament of the enemy consisted of six 11-in. guns and they were mounted in two turrets—one forward and the other aft. These turrets could be swung round to a certain angle but the control-tower, funnel and other necessary deck structures prevented the for'ard turret firing astern and the aft turret from firing ahead. The forward one could turn to about 60 degrees aft and the after one the same degree forward.

Immediately below the turrets was a space called the working chamber and from this ran a central tube some twelve feet in diameter going right to the bottom of the ship. As the turret swung so all those units turned with it. To load one of the guns a cordite charge was taken from the magazine, which was almost at the bottom of the ship and close to the central tube, and placed in the tray of a hoist in the central tube. A shell was then placed in another tray in the same hoist and they were hoisted up to the working chamber. In the working chamber were shelves fitted to take both shells and charges where they were stacked ready to be placed in another hoist which took them to the breech of the gun when required. This hoist fetched up immediately behind the gun.

Although "flash doors" are fitted to the working chambers to prevent sparks or flames finding their way to the magazine down the central tube they are not always effective in action.

A modern ship in action shows no outward sign of the intense activity taking place between decks and behind armour plating. In *Exeter* men were peering through long-range-finders and ascertaining distances between the ships engaged. This information was passed direct to the transmitting room which was really the nerve centre of the ship.

In the control-tower officers were busy spotting the fall of the shells and changing the range and deflection accordingly. Others were computing the speed and course of the enemy which were altering frequently as also were the speed and course of the *Exeter*. All this information was being passed every moment to the transmitting room. In that room was a large screen on which were two small model ships—one the *Exeter* and the other the enemy. These models were moved mechanically on the varying courses and speeds as passed down to the officer and he was thus able to see on the screen the constantly varying range and pass the distance to the gun-layers.

In the bowels of the *Exeter* men were stripped to the waist or wearing an old suit of dungarees. Some were in pyjamas, so hot was it in spite of the electric fans. Shells and bags of cordite were being carried to the ammunition hoist and were carried up to the working chamber where men were stacking them ready for loading.

In the turret there was a marked calmness. The variations were passed from the transmitting room by speaking tube and the gunner's mate had his ear always to the earpiece. The gun-layer stood on the steel platform peering through the telescopic sight, his finger on the trigger of the firing pistol. Rapidly he spun the brass wheel round to obtain the necessary elevation. His mate spun another wheel to get the deflection. Suddenly the gun-layer saw between the cross-wires in his telescope the grey hull of the enemy. Almost instinctively his finger pressed the trigger. There was a dull roar and the gun and platform swung back with the recoil. *Exeter* had opened fire.

The officers in the conning-tower watched the shells throw up their spouts of white foam. All fell short and the guns were at the utmost elevation. The ship was not yet in range, although the shells of the enemy were falling all round *Exeter*. Only one thing to do; alter course and come into range. This meant exposing the ship to enemy shells while still unable to reply, but it would not be for long. The order to alter course and get into range was passed to the navigating officer.

The next salvo brought a shout from the men in the conning-tower. The shells had straddled the enemy—they were in range and on their target.

And then, Crash!

Before the reverberations of that last salvo were lost the ship seemed almost to stagger in her course. There was a dull roar and the old hands knew that it was not the sound of one of their own guns firing. A shell from the enemy had burst somewhere in the ship.

In fact two shells had pierced the deck and burst below, perilously close to the petrol supply. Had that caught fire it would have been a terrible disaster. Fire at sea is dangerous at any time but it is fearful during action. Petrol burns with such a fierce heat and spreads with such rapidity that it seems to render everything it touches combustible; steel and iron appear to burn like dry wood.

Men were working in the chamber beneath the for'ard turret when the shell burst. There was no place to take cover; anyway, there would have been no time. Some who saw it burst into the chamber instinctively threw their arms over their head as a protection and others that had their backs to it were almost blinded by the fierce light in that small chamber. Every fixture was blown from its setting and became a dangerous missile along with flying splinters of steel. All lights were extinguished and all that could be seen in the darkness were pieces of red hot shell sizzling as they seared through the deck. Men were hurled against bulkheads or thrown to the deck. The noise of the explosion seemed to burst the ear drums and eyes were blinded by the fierce light.

It was some minutes before men could see again. In the blackness were heard the cries of the wounded and the groans of the dying. It was almost more than a human being could endure and remain sane. The concussion caused by the explosion made breathing difficult and men could be heard breathing in rasping sobs.

After what seemed an eternity one man recovered sufficiently to act. It was Engine-Room Artificer J. McGarry who, after being thrown against a bulkhead and knocked unconscious by the force of the explosion, slowly regained consciousness. He remembered that he was in charge of the men in this compartment.

Struggling to his feet he peered through the gloom and saw some of his shipmates lying dead and horribly mutilated. Others were terribly injured but mercifully unconscious. Others not so badly damaged were moaning and nursing their wounds.

He remembered with satisfaction that before the commencement of the action he had taken every precaution. He had noticed that the petrol compartment might become a source of danger in the event of a bursting shell. There was no time to consult his senior officer so he had flooded this compartment himself. His foresight had saved the ship from serious danger for the shell had exploded nearby and his action had prevented serious fire.

The cries of the wounded roused him to action. The nearest accident station was some distance away but the stricken men needed immediate attention. He improvised stretchers from parts of the battered compartment and called for volunteers to carry them to the sick bay. It was a very difficult job. It required courage to move about when a modern ship is in action. Although a man's intelligence may tell him that an enemy shell could easily penetrate the cover he has taken the very fact that he is sheltered seems to hold him to that spot. To venture out even below deck requires a decided mental effort. But when a man's objective is to assist wounded comrades thought of self vanishes.

Almost before McGarry had finished his call for volunteers men were at work lifting the shattered men on to the improvised stretchers and lashing them securely.

The nearest dressing-station may be only a few yards away but to reach it is not just a question of walking along deck. When a ship is in action all water-tight compartments are closed by iron, water-tight doors. The ship becomes a collection of small sections connected only by devious routes up and down hatchways. On no account must the water-tight doors be opened.

The regulation service stretcher used in ships is made of bamboo slats strung together rather like a pliable Venetian blind. The patient is laid in this and securely bound to prevent him from slipping. At times the stretcher must be tipped almost vertically, so narrow are the hatchways.

After tending the wounded, McGarry now looked about to see what damage was done to the compartment, for the hole made by the bursting shell had allowed a certain amount of daylight to penetrate. He sent for a repair party of shipwrights. Then he prepared to tell his senior officer the extent of the damage, but at that moment the Engineer Officer entered the room. By this time McGarry was almost done. He just had sufficient strength to make a full report when he fell unconscious into the arms of a comrade.

Shot and shell were falling on every side. The enemy had now got the range and were taking every advantage of it. Captain Bell had to endeavour to outwit him by altering direction and speed, for his ship was getting severe punishment from the heavier armament of his foe.

Then it was that *Ajax* and *Achilles* came into action. They had been some miles west of the *Exeter* and were not seen by the enemy's captain until some time after he had opened fire. Now they were in range they opened fire with their 6-in. guns.

The raider replied by turning her secondary armament of 5.9's on them, meanwhile

continuing to concentrate on *Exeter* with her
11-in.

But the guns of the British cruisers were
telling on the enemy. Several direct hits were
scored on or near the water-line. The sea
was calm but if a swell had come up, or a rough
sea, those holes would have been a grave menace.
They could not be properly repaired in the heat
of battle.

The plan of action between the three British
ships formulated before the meeting was now
put into operation. The *Exeter* had borne the
brunt of the battle so far and now the two
smaller ships took up the fight with zest. They
harried the raider from the rear, presenting as
little as possible of their ships as target.

Orders were clanging on the telegraph almost
as quickly as they could be answered.

"Starboard Engines Full Ahead."

"Stop Port Engines."

"Starboard Engines Full Astern."

"Full Ahead."

The ships were zigzagging, slowing down,
then darting ahead; doing everything in their
power to elude the enemy guns.

The modern turbine-driven ships have none
of the clang and bustle of the older type of
reciprocating engines. There is a noticeable lack
of movement as the turbines are running inside

huge metal cases, but even so there is no lack
of tensity or atmosphere in the engine-room.
All are working below the water-line and in
a part of the ship which is most vulnerable to
torpedo attack. At any moment during action
the deck plates may suddenly bulge upward,
there may be a dull explosion followed immediately by an inrush of water when the hull
has been hit by a torpedo. Working under these
conditions makes for tensity of atmosphere.

Engineer Commander C. E. Simms was co-
ordinating the efforts of his officers and men in
the supreme effort. Some of his junior officers
were standing by the telegraph waiting for signals
from the bridge. Warrant Officers and Chief
Petty Officers were going about their duties with
a calmness born of years of discipline. To see
some of them thrusting their hands between
rapidly moving parts of the auxiliary machinery
in an effort to find out whether the bearings
were running hot would make a layman shudder.

In the boiler-room stokers were watching the
oil sprays and looking anxiously at the steam
guages. The hands in the dials of some were
already tapping the full pressure limit but the
bridge was asking for more steam. These men
could only know the trend of the battle from
reports carried to them by word of mouth or elec-
trically transmitted and broadcast descriptions.

In the ceaseless hum of the turbines these fellows carried on. A dull thud told them that the ship had been hit by a heavy projectile, a sudden lurch conveyed the news that she herself had fired another salvo. They could only visualize her movements—and hope.

In the turrets nothing could quench the good humour of the gun's crews. Every breath of good news brought a cheer from them. Every fresh instruction from the transmitting room was followed in a flash. They toiled stripped to the waist or garbed in old dungarees, some even in night clothes, in this atmosphere of grime and stench. As soon as a breech-block was opened after firing, the smell of exploded cordite clung to the confined space of the turrets. The hose was plunged immediately into the breech but still the fumes escaped from the long, lean barrels.

Singing, shouting, swearing they toiled on unseen, unknowing. All that was required of them were blind obedience and magnificent team work in an atmosphere of increasing hell.

A terrific crash and the *Exeter* almost stayed in her course. An 11-in. shell had hit the forward turret fair and square. The direct impact of 670 pounds of steel and high explosive on the armour plate of the turret buckled it up as if it were made of tin. The two 8-in. guns were

Wright & Logan

H.M.S. "ACHILLES."

smashed from their mountings and lay sprawling across the foc'sle. The two gun's crews in this turret were drawn from the marines, that fine body of men which a sailor describes as being "neither food, flesh, fowl, nor good red herring" for the simple reason that they are soldiers not sailors. From earliest times marines have been carried in ships of war, and to-day the Marines are the fighting soldiers carried for punitive work ashore or larger work if called upon.

The marines in this turret were in charge of Sergeant A. B. Wilde. As the guns were completely put out of action Wilde ordered the men to leave the gun-house.

One of his marines, W. A. Russell, had one arm smashed and the other blown off. Red arterial blood was spurting from the stump and the man was rapidly bleeding to death. Such a sight would turn the stomach of many men but Wilde saw only the danger. He picked up a piece of rope and calmly tied a tourniquet round the stump, just under the shoulder. Tighter and tighter he twisted until he saw the pulsing flow slowly subside and then cease. It was in time to save the fellow's life, and Russell remained on deck cheering his comrades and refusing further aid until the battle was over.

Wilde stepped inside the gun-house and was alarmed to see that fire had broken out and was rapidly gaining the upper hand. It was approaching the rammer of one of the guns which already had a charge of cordite in it. It was imperative that fire should not reach that charge, but the hosepipe for clearing the gun-barrel was smashed beyond hope of using. Something had to be done quickly. Wilde organized a chain of men from the nearest water faucet to the gun-house. Bucket after bucket of water was passed until the fire was quenched, but Wilde was taking no risks, he coolly picked up the charge of cordite and threw it over the side.

Splinters from this smash hit on the for'ard gun turret nearly wrecked the bridge, which was immediately above and astern. Captain Bell was on the bridge at that moment. His messenger on his one hand and a bridge boy on the other were killed instantly by splinters. Captain Bell was unscathed.

Commander R. B. Jennings who, throughout the action, controlled the main armaments, found that the main control was now out of action, and he transferred his activities to the after control, taking up a post almost over the muzzle of the guns, regardless of the exposure to blast.

Suddenly a 5.9 smashed the *Exeter's* steering-gear. For some moments the cruiser reeled and veered wildly. Swiftly the Chief Quartermaster,

Petty Officer W. E. Green, followed the Captain aft, and very soon the secondary steering-gear was fully manned. The Captain took the hand steering flat and with a small boat's compass he steered the ship from there. There were no telegraphs to the engine-room from the aft hand steering, and so a chain of marines was organized to convey messages to the Engineer Commander.

But the *Exeter* had to face further damage before success came. Fire broke out, and fire at sea is a nightmare. Behind the sheets of steel is an arsenal. Magazine after magazine is crammed with cordite, gun-cotton and nitroglycerine.

An 11-in. shell had burst above an ammunition locker and set it alight, and Midshipman A. Cameron with great foresight ordered two guns' crews to take shelter. Almost immediately the locker exploded, but only a few of the second crew were wounded, and the midshipman's action undoubtedly saved many lives.

The explosion ignited another locker, and as soon as the main fire abated, with the help of Able Seaman W. G. Gwilliam he smothered the flames of the burning woodwork. The two of them then threw the unexploded shells over the side. They were still hot, and the brass cartridge-cases were either missing or split open.

Able Seaman Gwilliam also put out fires on the upper deck near the aircraft from which petrol was leaking.

Another Midshipman, R. W. D. Don, was working heroically in running hoses into the marines' barracks which was blazing, and in fighting another fire over the lower steering position.

The coolness and resource of all the Midshipmen were typical of the spirit ruling throughout the ship.

Acting Petty Officer H. V. Chalkley found his chance when an 11-in. shell burst in the Chief Petty Officer's flat above the dynamo-room. This is a key point in a ship. From its many switches the lighting of the whole ship is worked, and many of the smaller pieces of machinery obtain their motive force from the dynamo-room. All the ammunition hoists, from which the guns are served, depend upon the dynamo-room.

Chalkley was in the dynamo-room when the shell burst. He managed to open the door in the escape trunk and crawl over the wreckage to the switchboard hatch. He could not clear the wreckage away and, realizing that he could no longer be of assistance in the dynamo-room, he scrambled up the escape trunk to the upper deck, returned to the flat and helped the fire parties to get the fire under control and to isolate circuits so that the paralysis of the lighting services and of the electrically-served machinery was reduced to the minimum.

This vital work was carried out in conditions of great distress and physical ordeal.

Down in the sick bay heroism of another sort was continually apparent. Here the ship's doctor and his staff, reinforced by stretcher parties of non-executive ratings, were busy with the casualties. Some were too grave to be moved and to them the medical officer or an assistant must go. Meantime, every sort of casualty was being attended to, from major amputations to surface wounds, suffocations, burns. Swiftly injections were given to relieve the pain. The supplies of morphine sulphate were precious.

Sick Berth Chief Petty Officer C. D. Pope, was returning from the fore part of the sick bay where he had been sent to reinforce supplies when he was knocked unconscious by a shell bursting nearby. When he came to, the bottles with the precious drug were smashed, but his one thought was for the wounded men, and he groped back through the smoke and fumes to find some morphia ampoules which would serve the original purpose for which he was sent.

Back in the sick bay he ignored his own disaster and encouraged everyone with his optimism and kept them spirited, even when the sick bay itself was flooded.

One of the sick berth attendants, E. T. Dakin, had only been on *Exeter* a week, having been lent from *Ajax*, his first ship. Even so, he fitted in with the team perfectly. His first-aid treatment won commendation, and his initiative in the face of recurring difficulties was an inspiration to the wounded. Suddenly there was a rush to the aircraft which, all ready for flight, were still in their catapults because there had been no opportunity for using them. From the first instant of battle, pilots had been standing by ready to resist any raid by air that might come from the enemy. But none came, and visibility was so good that the extra field given to a battleship by the reports from her air arm was not necessary.

Shrapnel and splinters had damaged the planes, petrol tanks were leaking dangerously and there was fire close to. Acting Leading Airman E. A. Shoesmith, although his clothing was soaked in petrol, climbed on top of the centre section of one of the 'planes and cleared the triatic stay which had fallen across it. This in itself was a difficult feat, but with heavy leakage of petrol, his petrol-soaked clothes and the crucial danger of instant ignition from the flash of guns firing alongside, the peril was intense.

114

The jettisoning parties on both catapult platforms worked in dangers that were acute. Any moment gunfire, a spark, even a red-hot splinter from a bursting shell might turn the whole scene into a sheet of unquenchable flame.

Captain Bell tried everything. From the aft steering wheel he ordered the torpedo tubes to be brought into action. Commander C. J. Smith, who had to cope with the difficulties of broken and emergency communications, gave orders to port the helm and bring the ship into such a position that the torpedoes could be launched. Time after time the complicated manœuvre was calculated and carried out, but the raider managed to elude their passage, and Commander Smith and Petty Officer C. F. Hallas, the torpedo gunner's mate in charge, both of whom were wounded, then worked ceaselessly on repairs and fires.

H.M.S. *Exeter* was indeed sorely battered, and her crew were beginning to feel the strain of the intense cannonade. Her numbers were gravely depleted. Her brilliant gunnery in the face of superior armaments deserved greater success than the many minor hits that she had so far achieved on the raider.

Suddenly the commander in the aft control-tower, still braving the blast of the near muzzles, sent down the most welcome news of all. The raider had been hit full square in her control-tower from which were operated her main armaments. This was indeed a blow between the eyes. From now onwards her main armaments had to fire independently and more or less blindly. Range-finders were out of action, transmitting gear destroyed, key men must have been killed and co-ordination completely disorganized. No one shell could have had more paralysing effect than did this hit on the main control-tower of the raider.

Its effects were soon apparent. *Exeter*, gravely crippled, but still full of fight, was thankful for the relief of less frequent firing from the raider, and less accurate range. She knew, too, that her sister ships, *Ajax* and *Achilles* could now bear the brunt of the fight.

In the early part of the action they had been out of range and out of sight of the raider. In the last few exchanges they had come into sight and done what they could with their 6-in. guns. The raider, satisfied that she had almost put the *Exeter* out of action, was at first undismayed by the appearance of the smaller cruisers. Her captain knew their armaments and his advantage over them before they could get within effective range. They should not be difficult to account for when the heavier guns of the *Exeter* were silenced. But *Exeter* had the last word. That blow between the eyes was paralysing. It was the complete counter to the destruction that the raider had undoubtedly wrought on her opponent. But the Captain of the raider was too experienced a fighter to allow confused thinking to be the outcome of paralysis. The sight of three ships decided him. His own fuel was desperately low. His losses were very heavy. And he was by no means satisfied that he had completely silenced the *Exeter*.

Swiftly he made his decision to run for the shelter of neutral waters. He had less than 200 miles to go, but he had all the day before him because the action with *Exeter* had taken less than an hour and a half. At seven-thirty that morning the German commander headed for safety.

The fast British cruisers, *Ajax* and *Achilles*, had other ideas. For them the fight had scarcely started. They had no fears of the raider's superior armaments. They knew that their speed was faster. If the raiding lion was limping for home they were after an audacious kill.

CHAPTER VI

RETREAT IN DARKNESS

ALMOST as the first shot from the German raider screamed over H.M.S. *Exeter* news flashed round the world that a naval action had begun.

It was the *Admiral von Scheer*, messages said, and the British cruisers were *Exeter*, *Ajax* and *Achilles*.

In some news flashes the first intimation of the engagement was that H.M.S. *Achilles* had been sunk. But this report was at once denied by the Admiralty.

At that time, indeed, *Achilles* was not in action.

But it was not long before the two smaller cruisers were striving to get within range. The German pocket battleship had not completely silenced the *Exeter*, after ninety minutes' intense action. She had concentrated her main fire upon her, but meantime suffered incessant bombardment from the two lighter British cruisers.

Now the havoc wrought by the smaller vessels was increasing alarmingly.

Captain Langsdorff took stock anew. He swept his glasses to the south'ard. He weighed the opposition of the *Exeter* which was reducing speed. He had silenced many of her guns. She was in sore straits, but there was no indication that her fighting spirit was quenched. She was blazing away with every available gun, and he had grim proof of her marksmanship around him. He had dodged her torpedoes, sometimes more by luck than calculated movement. His control-tower was smashed, its key men were dead or severely injured. He was holed on the water-line. One hole in her bow was nearly five feet across. Shrapnel had brought innumerable casualties. The welded sides of his ship were peppered with holes. His aircraft were severely crippled.

He was in little better shape than *Exeter*, but confident that he could meet any further challenge from the British cruiser. But when he looked beyond the *Exeter* his decision was made. The two fast cruisers, *Ajax* and *Achilles* were now well within range. At the main of *Ajax* flew the broad pennant of the Commodore and the White Ensign of the Royal Navy.

Strength and confidence were in every line of them. Their speed was an indication of their determination.

So far they had been comparatively undamaged, though the raider's secondary armaments had been trained on them whenever they could be diverted from *Exeter*. Now, with his superior main armaments uncontrolled, the German commander had little advantage over the guns of the two smaller cruisers. They were still blazing away at him with their 6-in. guns and their marksmanship was dangerously accurate.

The German's response was crippled by the destruction of the control-tower and the British cruisers were zigzagging with bewildering speed.

Captain Langsdorff decided to run for it. He could not face the British trio with any hope of victory. He was dangerously short of fuel. His ship was a raider, and as such it was his duty to keep her afloat and, after repairs in neutral waters, to resume his plundering. The chances were at least even that he could slip out after dark, and with his main armaments repaired he could face the small British cruisers before reinforcements arrived.

If he fought, and lost, the sinking of his 10,000-ton ship could have no material effect upon the outcome of the war for Germany, but if he won the continued presence of the pocket battleship as a raider would certainly have a very considerable effect upon the economic strategy of the campaign. He had abundant evidence not only of the tonnage of food he was able to way-lay, but of the shipping that refused to set sail when his presence in near waters was made known.

Further, he had thoughts for his men. Almost all his crew, of nearly a thousand, were young-sters. They had never expected to face a battle, but they had done finely under fire.

He would save them and save his ship . . . if he could cover the 150 miles which were still between him and the protection of neutral waters.

But they were evidently going to be desperate miles to cover. The British cruisers gave him no rest.

Commodore Harwood's plan of action was clear cut. It had all been arranged before the enemy was sighted. The crippling of *Exeter* did not alter the strategy.

Captain Woodhouse, *Ajax*, and Captain Parry, *Achilles*, and their Commanders, Captain D. H. Everett and Commander D. M. L. Neame, had worked for months on the perfection of organiza-tion and personnel for the supreme test of action against a vastly superior foe.

At all costs they must avoid the risk of a broadside from the raider. Equally it would be folly to attempt to cut the battleship off from neutral waters, because such a manœuvre would make them dangerously vulnerable. The scheme, which was immediately put into operation with audacity, was to harry the raider, taking advantage of the superior speed of the British cruisers, to zigzag and to bombard her with the minimum risk of retaliation.

Swiftly the British cruisers began to lay smoke-screens to cover each other's movements. As *Ajax* darted ahead, burning crude oil was sprayed from the aft nozzles on to the sea, where it spread like a heavy, black pall. With a sudden burst of speed *Ajax* escaped from its cover and *Achilles* took immediate advantage of it. She, in her turn, laid another screen—into which *Achilles* entered and manœuvred.

The targets of the enemy raider were therefore changing with bewildering uncertainty. Her armaments, already hampered by the destroyed control, were gravely handicapped. The range-finders, robbed of precise calculation and co-ordination, found it almost impossible to pass accurate information to the turrets. The smoke-screens drifted and merged, but when and where the British cruisers would enter or leave them was beyond the anticipation or the calculation of the Germans.

Suddenly, as *Ajax* emerged from her dark cloud, there was a crash that seemed to silence the continual firing of her 6-in. batteries.

It was a hit by the German 11-in. gun on the cruiser's fore turret.

The blow momentarily staggered her.

The shell passed through the working chamber of the turret where Lieut. I. D. De'Ath, of the Royal Marines, was in charge.

The hatch of the chamber was blown open and sparks and smoke were pouring from it. At any moment the ammunition might explode, but the officer went at once to the hatch to ascertain the damage and to give immediate orders to ensure the safety of the ammunition.

The terrific impact and explosion destroyed communications, shattered electrical gear and added darkness to the horrors of fire, making rescue work a ghastly ordeal and first-aid a triumph of organization, backed by rare courage.

Severely wounded men refused all but primary attention until they had finished directing repair parties, stunned men picked themselves up and gave a hand. At all costs the service to the guns must not fail, must not even falter for a moment.

A.B.s took on the work of wounded officers; stokers, mechanics, shipwrights, marines worked with astonishing speed to repair the damage and to safeguard the ship.

Lieut.-Commander D. P. Dreyer, the gunnery officer, coping with the destruction from the shell and with the damage to the controls, maintained a magnificently effective fire and was prompt to co-operate in the most daring strategy when the pocket battleship began to put out a smoke-screen, behind which she at first partially and then completely disappeared.

Ajax was already full out, but the bridge rang down for still more speed.

Everyone in the engine-room responded; in the stokeholds response was simultaneous. Faith in the already hard-pressed engines and boilers was complete. Little thought was given to the gauges. For some time they had been registering a full head of steam, but it was a case of "All out! Let her go!"

Engineers and stokers, whose contact with the battle was through the orders from the bridge telegraph and from the recoil of their own firing, fought valiantly for more and more speed.

Ajax did thirty-four . . . thirty-six . . . thirty-eight knots. It seemed incredible, but she reached thirty-eight and held it.

She headed straight for the enemy's smoke-screen and reached its cover without being hit.

Once in the dark pall she did not slacken, but altered course and swiftly emerged into the sunlight—to find herself within a mile of the raider. Within a mile, when a broadside might have blown her almost out of the water.

Here was a chance to try a torpedo attack.

From the control came the order to the torpedo flat: "Discharge torpedoes!"

The torpedoes were already in the tubes. Quickly the Torpedo Officer adjusted the valves to the details of depth, range and distance which were transmitted to him. The propellers of the torpedoes were already slowly turning in the tubes.

"Close water-tight doors!"

The inside doors of the torpedo tubes were swung to and slammed with their own weight. The bolts shot home. A swift turn of the handles and the outside water-caps were opened. The sea rushed in and the torpedoes—each now a ship in its own right—responded immediately to their own element. The propellers bit upon the water and the miniature submarines were slowly propelled along the tubes by their own power.

As soon as they lost the protection of the tubes the rush and weight of the sea knocked the cocks "full on" and away they sped on their planned journey.

In the bright light of the summer morning Captain Langsdorff and his look-outs did not miss the tell-tale trail of bubbles. By swift manœuvring he avoided a direct hit. One torpedo from *Ajax* passed within ten feet of his bows and while he was avoiding this new menace he suffered considerable damage from the *Ajax's* for'ard 6-in. guns.

Ajax turned and doubled on her tracks without reducing speed and the sudden turn drove her fo'c'sle-head completely under the water.

For a moment she took it green.

Watchers in the control-tower saw the water sweep over the for'ard guns which were almost red hot and, as the cruiser shook herself free of the sea, the long, gaunt barrels reappeared, no longer grey, but black and steaming.

Off dashed *Ajax* into the nearest smoke-screen and laid another while she turned her narrow stern to the raider. The agile manœuvring called for the most complete co-ordination of effort and complete understanding between the two ships.

The perfection of team-work survived an early disaster to *Achilles*.

Several heavy splinters struck the gun-director tower. Three men were killed and two injured inside the tower.

Lieut. R. E. Washbourn was half stunned. The man beside him was killed, but the lieutenant continued to control the main armament with amazing coolness. His courage was reflected in his team who stood to their posts, making light of the incident. Sergeant S. J. Trimble, of the Royal Marines, was one of those severely wounded, but he stood fast without flinching or complaint. The guns must be served and there must be no pause.

Gunner Watts, the rate officer, carried on through the fierce firing, and when his rate-keeping was no longer required, tended the wounded without thought for his own danger.

Lieut. G. S. Cowburn, when his commanding officer was wounded, handled the ship with remarkable skill and gave a running commentary on the progress of the action which was broadcast to all positions between decks, including the engine-room, and did much to facilitate perfect team-work. Men in all parts of the ship were braced by his encouragement and spurred to new effort by this opportunity of visualizing the results of their labours and the success of their work.

The signals that passed between *Achilles* and *Ajax* were visual. The Chief Yeoman of Signals, L. C. Martinson, handled a team whose great zeal and proficiency was a feature of the battle. New Zealanders brought their fine peace record for signalling undamaged and even enhanced through the heat of action.

Suddenly the Chief Yeoman of Signals was

injured by shrapnel. So far, by artful manœuvring, *Achilles* had avoided major hits— but she suffered severely from shrapnel. The heroism of Boy A. M. Dorset flashed round the ship. With dead and wounded about him he never faltered in maintaining his vital link in the chain. He passed such information as was available to him to the guns and repeated their reports clearly and swiftly to the gunnery officer.

Achilles was firing continual broadsides. The strain was intense, the noise shattering, but the men stood up to it magnificently. They had no thought for themselves, no thought even for food. They ate if they could, if and when food was brought to them.

The sick bays were now full and temporary first-aid stations were set up when wounded could not be moved or could not be extricated from the destruction.

The Principal Medical Officer was a New Zealander, Surgeon-Lieut. C. G. Hunter—a young man to hold such a position, with its crucial responsibilities in action.

Suddenly he was faced not only with minor casualties but with urgent major operations in large numbers, and his judgment in dealing with them and his remarkable gifts of organization did much to keep the mortality aboard *Achilles* at such a low figure.

Wright & Logan

H.M.S. "AJAX"

Now *Ajax* took up the running.

Lieut. E. D. G. Lewin begged to be given the opportunity to spot from his aeroplane, which was standing ready in the catapult, but had been damaged early in the action.

Captain Woodhouse was very doubtful whether the craft was airworthy; indeed, its obvious damage was such that a flight must be extremely hazardous, but the help that the pilot, from his vantage-point above—in spotting the falling of the shots—would be invaluable to the cruiser. His radio telephone information would enable the range-finders to adjust their calculations by results.

The pilot rose swiftly, circled and approached the raider. For an hour or more he was an extra eye to the cruiser—a far-seeing eye.

He was in constant danger and immediately became the target of the raider's anti-aircraft guns, but he kept up his spotting until the condition of his aeroplane made return imperative.

In the heat of battle, when the cruiser was steaming at speed, he effected a safe landing, drew alongside, and was hooked inboard. The whole manoeuvre was executed with the calmness and precision of battle practice.

For hours through the morning the British cruisers fought with swift, terrier-like action, harassing the raider through every mile of her journey to neutral waters.

At high noon, after six hours of fierce fighting, there was a lull. The heat of the day made relaxation welcome, but there was little respite. Every minute was used to bring the damaged cruisers to the maximum efficiency. Clearly the fight was not finished and, while gun crews were able to relax, repair parties were working throughout the ship. Temporary repairs done in the heat of battle were made more permanent, ammunition hoists were re-oiled, guns cleaned.

Fierce fire-fighting was still going on in all parts, but in the sick bay it was possible to give more than first aid to the many casualties. As many cooks as could be spared were called back from the stretcher parties to their galleys and, under conditions very different from normal routine, a scratch meal was prepared and food distributed to those who still could not leave their posts.

The enemy allowed short respite, for the heat of the early afternoon was soon shattered by activity on the part of the raider—which was immediately countered by the British cruisers. The battle was on again, and there was no relaxation of its fierceness.

As the raider approached the Uruguayan shore and the British cruisers continued their tactics,

the fight clearly developed into a contest of
brains and dexterity versus superior power.
For miles there was now a pall of smoke from
the continual use of smoke screens which drifted
and merged, and from the heavy smoke belching
from the funnels of three ships that were steaming
at utmost speed.

As the afternoon drew on, the battle scene
assumed grim majesty. On both sides was
evidence of relentless purpose. For hours the
British cruisers schemed for position and wrought
what damage they could. Their tactics compelled the raider to alter course so repeatedly
that she lost time and doubled the length of her
journey to safety.

As the sun dropped, the British cruisers
utilized to the full the shadow and confusing
detail of the land and positioned themselves
so that the enemy was silhouetted against the
luminous sunset sky.

Although there was still much light in the
sky this clever dispositioning of the British
cruisers gave them almost the cover of darkness.
The enemy was now a fine target, whereas they
were enjoying the natural camouflage of the
varied background of the Uruguayan coast.

It was clear from the faltering gunfire of the
raider that she was at a disadvantage. She
had little more than the gun-flashes from the

British cruisers upon which to work for a range. Her accuracy faltered. Meantime there were continual broadsides from *Ajax* and *Achilles* at a target which was silhouetted completely against the sky.

There was something symbolic in the now reduced steaming of the battered raider into the fading light of the sunset.

She was now within grasp of safety. Her Commander had achieved his end, but at a price that still could not be computed. He had been out-manœuvred, out-gunned, out-steamed, in a running fight from dawn to sunset.

Still he did not relax, and every broadside from the almost invisible cruisers was answered.

Suddenly the battleship turned. News of the raider's movement spread swiftly through the British ships. It was inconceivable that she could contemplate a dash for the open sea; the British captains were confident that she was desperately short of oil, but whatever she proposed to do they were ready for her. After worrying her for fifteen hours they were not relaxing their grip now.

Swiftly the reason for the raider's manœuvre was apparent. As she swung round she fired a final broadside; every available gun was brought into this last desperate salvo. In the twilight the flashes of the raider's guns lit up the whole scene. The booms seemed to reverberate to and fro across the estuary. Then there was an almost terrifying silence.

Slowly, almost wearily, the raider resumed her course and steamed into the sanctuary of neutral waters.

For her the fight was finished, at least for a while, but for the British cruisers there could be no relaxation. For them danger was still imminent. The Captains of the British cruisers were too experienced in naval warfare to underrate the possibilities of the apparently stricken enemy.

The drama of tense action had ceased, but the strain of vigilance was still acute. The exhausted and depleted crews, inexpressibly weary in the reaction after the fight, had to face hours of repair work and the strain of unceasing watch.

Armourers cut away the twisted steelwork and replated the damaged turrets. Mechanics straightened out the twisted tubes of rangefinders and tested them anew. Electricians searched for torn mains and replaced temporary repairs by work that might well have to stand the strain of further action in the morning. In the magazines, shells were being closely stacked close to the ammunition hoists. Empty cases were cleared away and the bags of cordite replenished.

In the engine-room engineers and stokers gave themselves little time for relaxation. They congratulated each other on the magnificent results they had secured from the engines and boilers, but even now the stokers were testing the oil-burners, cleansing the cocks, and generally getting back into battle trim—in case they were called upon for a repetition of the day's performance.

In the sick bays a more silent repair party was doing its work. The doctor and his assistants were giving the casualties detailed attention; the padre was ministering to those who hovered near death.

Some of the sick bay staff were laying out the dead, and silently their comrades watched the bodies being covered with the flag for which they had died, but not in vain.

CHAPTER VII

AT BAY

WHEN the German pocket battleship steamed slowly through neutral waters there was a ripple of doubt through the massed crowds as to whether she could enter the difficult port of Montevideo. The wharfs were black with people and flat-roofed houses round the harbour were used as grand stands. All through the afternoon every approach road had been jammed with traffic and pedestrians. The shallow waters were alive with small craft. Everywhere, even in the late evening hours, there was an atmosphere of tense excitement but no jubilation. The drama of the seas seemed to have conveyed itself to the hundreds of thousands of people who had gathered to see what they could of the last hours of the fight and of the incoming of the German battleship.

There were no lights on the raider as she approached the port, but the luminous night was sufficient to reveal her shattered outline.

She did not stop to pick up a pilot. With the usual thoroughness of the German Navy, she had presumably among her reserve officers a man who had a pilot's certificate for the River Plate.

Meantime *Ajax* and *Achilles* hovered outside the line of neutral waters. They had followed the battleship all the way to Montevideo, but did not enter the harbour.

For the raider the fight had temporarily ceased, but for the British cruisers there could be not a moment's relaxation. Unlike her, they were still in belligerent waters. They might meet German naval units, a submarine whose torpedo might destroy all the gains of the day's battle, or even the ravages of a raid by air. They did not anticipate the arrival of substantial German reinforcements in time, but a speeding battleship, sensing the hopelessness of her quest, might well launch her aircraft in an endeavour to strike at the British cruisers which held the German raider at bay.

The drama of tense action had gone, but there could be no relaxation; not a moment's respite while the raider remained above water. The men faced an ordeal hardly less severe than that of the past twelve hours.

In an atmosphere of immeasureable weariness, with the losses of the battle now translated into personal terms, and with the mental languor that follows heavy physical strain, the men drove themselves to the activities now demanded of them. But they disciplined themselves with a will. Their bodies and minds might be weary but their spirit was triumphant. Their heads were still aching from the sound of the guns; their eyes still unaccustomed to the night. The blinding flash of gunfire seemed continually before them; their limbs seemed reluctant to obey any but the orders they had been fulfilling for hours. Many found themselves momentarily helpless; without complete and instant control over their limbs. Some staggered like drunken men. But they laughed and sang in their discomfort. Words of praise had already come from the officers who had set them such a fine example in the fight. They knew they had done a good day's work. They were satisfied. On the raider's decks, they knew, like conditions were occurring, but there the weariness could not be banished by the gladness of victory. It would be made doubly acute by the humiliation of retreat and the prospect of facing ultimate defeat.

The 10,000-ton £4,000,000 pocket battleship, still assumed to be the *Admiral von Scheer*, swung at anchor during the night.

With the first rays of dawn intense activity began. As soon as the port authorities boarded the German raider some doubts were cast upon her identity. Some of the British prisoners had seen what they thought were the permanently embossed letters *Admiral von Scheer* upon her stern. When the German authorities returned to the city, however, they announced authoritatively that the raider was not the *Admiral von Scheer* but the *Admiral Graf Spee*, which name, although painted out, could still be read distinctly on her stern.

The question that now transcended all other considerations was how long the raider would be allowed to stay, what repairs could be effected in the time, and what would be her fate when she left the shelter of neutral waters.

The position was made clear in the House of Lords by Admiral of the Fleet Lord Chatfield, Minister for the Co-ordination of Defence. He said: "The international law was laid down in the Hague Convention No. 13. It provided that a belligerent vessel could not remain in a neutral port for more than twenty-four hours, except in certain circumstances; that a belligerent vessel might prolong its stay on account of damage or stress of weather, and must depart as soon as the delay was over; and that such vessels might carry out only repairs to render them seaworthy and might not add in any manner whatever to their fighting force. The local authorities of the neutral Power decided what repairs were necessary, and these had to be carried out with the least possible delay.

"I have no doubt," the Admiral concluded, "that the *Graf Spee* will soon be at sea again—for a short time."

Then began a diplomatic tussle between the interests concerned. The German Legation immediately made formal requests to the Uruguayan Government for permission to keep the *Graf Spee* in port long enough to carry out sufficient repairs to make her "seaworthy."

The British Government made representation to the Government of Uruguay, pointing out that the raider ought to be compelled to put to sea again within twenty-four hours. The British Government also pointed out that as the *Graf Spee* reached Montevideo under her own steam and at appreciable speed the question of "seaworthiness" did not arise and therefore there was no reason why she should not put to sea again in a similar condition.

Expert examinations were made of the damaged raider and, while opinions differed as to the length of time required for repairs and as to the necessity for sending to Buenos Aires for special parts (which was made the cause of a plea for further delay), all were agreed upon the amazing extent of the damage inflicted by the smaller British cruisers.

Naval experts hailed the action as a triumph for British gunnery and a vindication of the theory that smaller guns of higher frequency, properly handled, are more than a match for larger calibre armaments.

It was vital to British interests and indeed consonant with International Law that the raider should be forced to leave her sanctuary within a day, or two days at the outside. The International Law was never framed to give time for the reconditioning of armaments, or for the summoning of reinforcements; its terms providing solely for breathing space in which to make a ship seaworthy but not necessarily battleworthy. It would have suited Germany's hand to have had several weeks' respite. Indeed, there is no doubt that an even longer period would have been necessary to put the raider into good battle shape. But the raider had been vanquished in fair fight, and the British were waiting to complete their kill.

It would have been a travesty of justice if the sanctuary of neutral waters had been exploited to permit the German raider to escape and to operate again after the heavy sacrifices that had been made by the British to sweep her from the seas.

Eventually all arguments were settled by the announcement by the Uruguayan Government that the *Graf Spee* would be allowed seventy-two hours from the time that she reached Montevideo, after which she would surrender herself to internment or leave Uruguayan waters.

In the latter event she would again have to face the British cruisers *Ajax* and *Achilles*, still patrolling ceaselessly across the estuary. Dawn had revealed the presence of the stricken *Exeter*, which, though gravely damaged by the brunt of the fight, had steamed up to take her place in whatever action arose from the raider's attempt to leave.

Meanwhile, in an atmosphere of growing tension, the raider attended to her sombre duties. Launches took her dead ashore. The crew stood at the salute.

At the funeral service, taken by a German pastor, were many of the British merchant captains who had been prisoners in the *Graf Spee*. Captain G. Pottinger attended as the official representative of the prisoners and laid a wreath bearing the inscription "To the memory of brave men of the sea, from their comrades of the British merchant service" on the German graves.

Captain Langsdorff's bearing at the funeral was impressive. For almost a minute he stood at the salute before each separate grave. He seemed lost to the world about him, oblivious of the strained uneasiness of the crowd.

It is not hard to realize the workings of his mind, for on every side there were tributes to his seamanship, personal courage and chivalry.

No men were more elated at the outcome of the battle than the British merchant captains, officers and crews who had been released in accordance with international law immediately the *Graf Spee* dropped anchor at Montevideo.

They had many tales to tell of their confinement in the raider and no complaints. One after another recorded Captain Langsdorff's frequently expressed claim that he would never willingly take a civilian sailor's life by his raids. It was his habit to apologize to the English merchant captains for actions that were forced upon him by the dictates of war. He treated them in the best tradition of seamanship, and gave them every consideration within his power.

Some of the captains recorded, with a certain amusement, the officiousness of a civilian decoding officer who was generally included in the boarding parties by which the British merchant vessels were searched. When he boarded the *Tairoa* and demanded, in not too perfect English, "Have you any secret papers?" he was disconcerted to receive the reply: "Oh, yes! Plenty!" He followed one Murphy to his

THE 5-FOOT HOLE IN THE BOWS OF THE "GRAF SPEE." THE INTERNAL
EXPLOSION HAS THRUST THE STEEL PLATES OUTWARDS,

cabin, who thereupon produced not secret but cigarette papers. The German decoding expert raged at what he chose to consider a deliberate impertinence, but was in fact an innocent misinterpretation of his imperfectly pronounced words.

Captain Langsdorff had issued standing instructions to the boarding officer that all chronometers and sextants should be brought aboard the *Graf Spee*. His instruction was also to collect any books that were found on the British merchantmen. These he stamped with the *Graf Spee* stamp, and formed them into a library for the use of the prisoners.

Langsdorff was a great reader himself and seemed particularly interested in books dealing with the activities of raiders during the Great War. It seemed to be a determination, almost an obsession, with him that whatever was subsequently written about the raiding activities of the *Graf Spee*, nothing could be legitimately held to his discredit.

Once or twice, when the British captains had their first interview with him, they asked for the return of their chronometers, but on this point the German captain was politely firm. "Winston Churchill," he said, "will buy you another one, but you may keep your watch."

This concession was typical of his consideration,

for, by setting their watches to the chronometers, the captains were enabled throughout the journey to estimate fairly accurately their longitude.

The British prisoners were also allowed to keep their money and to spend it in the ship.

The Master-at-Arms, Albert Jerichow, was in charge of the prisoners, who relieved the tedium of their confinement by games and reading, and other amusements which were not difficult to organize in view of the latitude allowed.

Frequently of an evening individual captains were invited by Langsdorff to his cabin for a chat. Politics and the world situation were discussed with complete frankness and freedom. The skippers found no evidence of a fanatic Nazi spirit, except that some of the younger members of the crew were quite convinced that if they were taken prisoners by the British their hands and their feet would be cut off.

There were some minor discomforts among the prisoners before their systems adjusted themselves to the unaccustomed food, but within a few days they became quite used to the meals and there was no shortage. The synthetic butter, however, worried some of the men—who found it more like chewing-gum in consistency.

On the morning of the 13th, when the British prisoners were suddenly locked in their quarters and the alarm sounded for the Germans to stand to their stations, there was plenty of speculation as to the reason for their complete confinement.

They knew from the activity aboard the raider that she had sighted another ship, but they were not left long in doubt that, in fact, the raider had sighted the British Navy.

Suddenly their speculations were shattered by a blinding flash and an ear-splitting crash, which caused many of them to reel and stagger and some of those still in their hammocks to be flung to the floor.

To many it was the greatest shock of their lives, but none had any doubt as to the cause. The midshipman's quarters, in which they were then housed, were below and slightly ahead of the for'ard turret—whose three 11-in. guns the prisoners had had ample opportunity to inspect.

Speculation began, not only as to the progress of the fight, but as to the ships engaged. The German commander had frequently boasted that he had no fears of the British Navy, except for the three battle cruisers *Hood*, *Repulse* and *Renown*, and these, he was satisfied, were not in near waters.

The prisoners, who were all experienced sea-men, had little difficulty in interpreting the movements of the ship and the sounds of the battle.

Sometimes the captives were thrown about as the pocket battleship suddenly turned in her course. She listed to such an extent that the men frequently slithered down the deck into the angle formed by the deck and the bulkhead. It was an uncomfortable experience against a background of incessant firing.

Frequently the din of gunfire was so terrific that it seemed that the German commander was firing every gun in the ship. The jar to the deck-head loosened dust and particles that filled the air and set many of them choking painfully.

But despite the discomfort and the danger, the excitement of the battle they could not see was so intense that it was many hours before the prisoners realized they had had no food that day. They began to share out the remains of the previous night's supper. Even the hard black bread was now welcome, but when a call was heard from the sentry outside: "Are you all right in there?" the cry was: "Yes, but we'd like some coffee!"

The request was not fulfilled. The prisoners subsequently learned that the galleys had been shot away by British shell-fire.

After some hours even the drama of the fight became monotonous and the fears that at any moment a torpedo from the British Navy might destroy them all became less acute. They even began the usual good-humoured arguments over games of cards and expressed indignation when a salvo momentarily made conversation impossible.

Suddenly there was a crash that could not be ignored, even by hardened listeners. Men were thrown from their chairs, cards scattered, there was a moment of chaos as the men disentangled themselves. All lights went out, parts of the deck-head fell in pieces about the players. Men grabbed their life-belts and put them on; some sustained minor injuries. There was general alarm. For some minutes men groped about in a fog of dust.

Gradually, as the ship came on an even keel and the atmosphere cleared, attempts were made to discover the exact damage caused by what must have been a direct hit by a very heavy shell.

A splinter from an earlier shell had torn away some of the bulkhead, and there was a scramble to the chink to see the damage.

There was a cheer when the damage was described by the observer. The gun within view had been shattered, and now lolled uselessly in a heap of twisted steel. Its crew were scattered; some lay wounded on the decks.

Cards were resumed; the helpless inactivity turned to boredom. Quite early in the evening men were climbing into their hammocks, dusting the debris from their bedding and deciding to sleep it out.

Opinion as to their chances of survival were divided. Some were impressed by the German captain's assurance that his ship was unsinkable; others thought that complete destruction might result at any minute. All regarded as their main danger the possibility of being torpedoed.

Late in the evening, when almost all were in bed, there was a sudden turning of the ship, followed by a fierce burst of firing. The men seemed unable to rid their ears of the noise. For hours, in their confined space, the air seemed to have been constantly reverberating. Nerves were taut, bodies were weary. The strain of uncertainty and helplessness was beginning to tell. Each gun-burst brought indignant shouts and curses. Then, in each lull, the exhausted prisoners dozed. They were almost beyond caring; their one desire was to be left alone.

Suddenly those who had found some sleep sat up; those who were awake were as suddenly alert. They were almost beyond hearing the wearing din of battle. It had become an inevitable background, even to their dreams, but a sudden, almost painful silence had descended with the touch of a switch.

"The engines have stopped!"

There was a burst of eager talk. Some were almost too exhausted to take any interest; others were full of possible explanations. There could be so many reasons, but only two mattered. Victory or defeat?

Suddenly the door of their quarters opened. A German officer, picking his way with a torch, said: "Gentlemen, for you the war is ended. We are now anchored in Montevideo Harbour."

The reaction was overwhelming, but doubts held back the feelings of the captives. They were too numbed to believe the news and men clambered to the skylight, peered through the chink made by the splinters, surged round the officer at the door.

Yes, they were in harbour. Lights could be seen in dazzling contrast to the total darkness of the ship. Someone who knew the Plate recognized the light of El Cerro flashing from the high building in the centre of the city.

It was true. They were certainly in harbour, and it was Montevideo.

Their conjectures as to the reason for this anchorage and its effect on themselves were put aside by the appearance of a steward with food.

Even in defeat, Captain Langsdorff had thought for his captives. The steward brought a message from the Captain who apologized for the lateness of the meal and the fact that it was cold. The whole ship's company were in the same difficulty; the galleys had been shot away. They were at the close of a desperate action.

But there was no malice or bitterness. Early the next morning the Master-at-Arms made his familiar call. There was no change in his bearing. One of the English skippers showed him a splinter of shell that had entered their quarters. The Master-at-Arms fingered it pensively and then with a smile said: "Made in England."

Several of the British prisoners had opportunity to meet their captor before they went ashore as free men. He expressed admiration for the fighting quality of the British ships and for their tenacity throughout the action. He said that against such brave foes there could be no personal enmity. His bearing was impressive and sincere, but many of the British captains who entertained for him a feeling of genuine admiration were shocked at his altered appearance after the strain of the action.

When they went ashore the British seamen were met by members of the British Legation who again informed them that they were free men. And not only free men, but favourites of the

Uruguayan people and the guests of the British and the French diplomatic officials.

The welcome contrast did much to ease the memories of their recent imprisonment, and they were immediately given facilities to communicate with their families at home. Many of them had had no news for months.

But even in their festivities they could not forget the battleship whose gaunt outline dominated the harbour of Montevideo. Whenever they forgathered they found themselves echoing the continual question:

"What will be the fate of the *Graf Spee*?"

In the House of Commons, the Prime Minister, Mr. Neville Chamberlain, in his review of the war on December 14, said: "At sea, the chief event has been the action which has taken place in South American waters. There is little that I can add at present to the reports which have already appeared.

"Shortly after six o'clock yesterday morning Commodore Harwood, in the 6-in. gun cruiser *Ajax*, reported that he was in contact with a German pocket battleship. Thereupon, in company with the 8-in. gun cruiser *Exeter* and 6-in. gun *Achilles*, he attacked the enemy, who made off in the direction of Montevideo.

"During the action, which was of a severe character, H.M.S. *Exeter* received damage which reduced her speed and forced her to drop out of the fight. The two 6-in. gun cruisers, however, continued the pursuit and at about midnight the German ship which turned out to be the *Admiral Graf Spee*, carrying six 11-in. guns, took refuge within territorial waters and is now anchored off Montevideo.

"A statement issued through the German Minister to Uruguay admitted that the *Admiral Graf Spee* has thirty-six dead and sixty wounded, and alleges that these losses were due to the use by the British cruisers of mustard gas. This characteristic statement is of course entirely without foundation. No gas shells or gas grenades have been made for or used by any ships of His Majesty's Navy.

"Although full details are not yet available, I think it is already apparent that a very gallant action has been fought by three comparatively small British ships against a much more heavily armed adversary, the result of which may well be to free the South Atlantic from the depredations of this raider."

The Premier's statement was punctuated by frequent prolonged cheers.

CHAPTER VIII

DEATH OF THE RAIDER

THE seventy-two hours in which the *Graf Spee's* decision had to be made, were hours of feverish activity.

Montevideo was the focus of the world. Each step in the diplomatic tussle was commented upon in every capital.

Langsdorff demanded more time for repairs, not, he insisted, to reinforce his armaments, but to make his ship seaworthy and not to endanger his crew. But his ship, the authorities pointed out, had come in under her own steam on the night of the 13th, and had suffered no further damage. The shortage of fuel and stores could be easily remedied within seventy-two hours.

Germany now took up the argument, even to the point of threats. But it soon became evident that the decision of the Uruguayan authorities was final. The question now was, how would the *Graf Spee* act.

It seemed impossible that she could fight her way out successfully, for the two British cruisers kept unceasing watch. The crippled *Exeter* was still there to bar the way; there was an announcement from the British First Lord of the Admiralty that powerful reinforcements were speeding to Montevideo, and the French battleship *Dunkerque* was known to be in near waters.

Even the most optimistic could not forsee any substantial German reinforcements appearing on the scene in time.

There were some who hoped that, according to the highest traditions of the German Imperial Navy, the *Graf Spee* might make for the open sea and go down fighting.

The more thoughtful could see no point in such an action because the glory would be outweighed by the serious loss of a capital ship and the unnecessary sacrifice of many lives.

Internment would mean impotence for the rest of the war and the possibility of a super-battleship, embodying many German naval secrets, passing to the hands of the enemy.

No one could fail to appreciate the acuteness of the problem. As Saturday passed it seemed to obsess the city which had taken on a strange appearance.

All business was at a standstill, except for the commercial elements that were exploiting the occasion. As soon as the time-limit had become known parties flocked in from all over Uruguay, excursions were run, hotels filled, temporary stands were erected on every available space. House roofs were let at fancy prices, ships and even aeroplanes were chartered to stand by for the final scene of the great sea drama.

There was the hustle of constant movement, the shouting of wares, the bright colours of the summer throng, but no cheering, and little gaiety. Whatever form the final drama might take it could not be dissociated from tragedy. There, before every watcher, was the stricken warrior. Her shattered control-tower broke the majesty of her fine lines. The shambles of her decks had been cleared, but the twisted steel, the gaping holes now boarded with planks, the riddled hull, were eloquent of defeat.

But it was defeat with honour, yet even honour was soon to be dimmed.

Swiftly rumour spread among the dense crowds that the German captain had made final appeal to Berlin.

For hours crowds waited round the German Legation. On Saturday they were rewarded by a sight of the German commander entering its doors. There was a murmur of sympathy as his drawn, grey face was studied. He had had little sleep and no rest for forty-eight hours.

With a typical exploitation of the dramatic it was conveyed to the crowd that Captain Langsdorff was to speak to the Fuhrer. He was at that moment taking the call that would bring Hitler's voice to his ears.

For a long time the crowd waited and when at last the German captain reappeared his expression conveyed no message save that it was etched with despair.

He returned to his hotel but it was not long before the Captain was back in the *Graf Spee*. She was the scene of intense activity. The cautiousness of the Uruguayan experts had resulted in urgent appeals to Buenos Aires. Now the crew of the German raider, supplemented by experts from Buenos Aires' engineering firms, swarmed over the ship like ants repairing a shattered ant heap.

Men on floats patched the damage near her water-line, cradles were slung over the side of the ship and the rattle of riveting echoed across the water like machine-gun fire. Here and there were stabs of vivid light as armourers with oxy-acetylene lamps cut away the twisted plates and reinforced the torn and battered hull.

Her aeroplanes were beyond hope of repair, apart from the fact that international law forbade any attempt to repair armaments; but to the astonishment of many, working parties were seen on staging erected outside the damaged control-tower. This, too, was contrary to the requirements of neutrality, but there could be

Fire rages from bow to stern on the "Graf Spee."

no mistaking the feverish efforts to restore the brains of the fighter.

The supply ship *Tacoma*, which had been lying in harbour, was ordered alongside and re-fuelling pipes were taken inboard the *Graf Spee* and oil pumped into her. It was known that when the raider dropped anchor she had only enough fuel in the tanks for a further thirty miles.

But now speculation began anew. Work parties were relieved and renewed. As Saturday passed the efforts seemed to be reaching their climax. There were rumours that temporary repairs would be completed by the night or at least sufficiently early on Sunday morning to make it possible for the raider to attempt a dash for safety under cover of darkness.

It was only a rumour among the crowds, but Uruguayan officials were so confident that this plan was intended that they took steps to control outgoing shipping from Montevideo. Measures were taken to prevent a congestion of shipping in the near waters during the night of Saturday. The crowd heard of these precautions and they confirmed their own reasonings. Surely the raider must be going to run the gauntlet, other-wise why this fierce effort to re-fill her tanks and to repair not only her sea-worthiness but her fighting strength?

The time limit expired at eight o'clock on Sunday night, local time; three and a half hours ahead of Greenwich mean time.

During the late afternoon of Saturday, however, a factor arose which the German command had not taken into account. The crew of the German pocket battleship refused to take their ship to sea. The revolt was not entirely unexpected because the revulsion of the young crew to the deaths and injuries of the battle had not been hidden. Apart from their inexperience of warfare the crew had been so steeped in Langsdorff's assurances that they would never be called upon to fight that the horrors of battle had been doubly shocking. Many of the British captains who were released at Montevideo were struck by the low state of the crew of the German raider and of the physical breakdown of many of the young men. They responded at first to the distraction of urgent labour in harbour, but when they realized the intentions of the Captain, and as zero hour approached, they no longer hid their feelings.

Their attitude was suspected by men aboard ships nearby in the harbour and late in the afternoon suspicions were confirmed by the sight of the crew mustered on deck. Officer after officer spoke to them, and when their sullen resentment did not respond to appeals, they were harangued.

Again and again the crew were mustered, watched by observers on naval and mercantile shipping moored in near waters. At each fresh assembly the spirit of rebellion seemed more resolute. At the later musterings there was little appearance of order. The men broke the ranks in such numbers that they appeared to be verging on a mutiny. There was shouting and disorderly behaviour.

At last Captain Langsdorff addressed his men. They had a warm regard for him. The crew listened more attentively, but their attitude was unchanged. Raiding had been exciting and for months the Captain's assurance that they would never be called upon to fight, had been kept. But the battle was etched on their minds in ghastly detail. They had had enough of war. They were not going to fight again.

Their Captain's final appeal did not alter their decision. They were dismissed at 7.30 p.m. and Langsdorff, after consultation with his officers, went ashore to confer with the German Minister. Meantime repairs proceeded. Thousands of gallons of oil were still pouring into the vast tanks of the pocket battleship.

The German Minister made fresh contact with Berlin. The German Captain waited. The fresh developments were put before the German Chancellor. They underlined in tragic fashion the grimness of defeat. Just before midnight there came to the nerve-racked and exhausted commander the order to scuttle his ship.

In the darkness he returned to the raider. He did not convey the Berlin instruction to the sullen crew, but he gave immediate orders that repair work was to be suspended. There was a hum of conjecture among the crew, but no certainty as to what it meant. They did not know that the Captain's next order was to make arrangements with Buenos Aires for two large German-owned Argentine tugs to tow a large barge over to receive the crew of the raider after she had been scuttled and to take them to Buenos Aires.

On Sunday morning the hundreds of thousands of watchers on land, at sea, and even in the air, were weary. To their surprise, as full daylight enabled them to get a clear view of the raider, there seemed to be a similar apathy on her decks. The watchers could not imagine that repair work had proceeded so swiftly as to be completed. There was still ample evidence of the destruction wrought in the battle and of the impermanence of many of the major repairs. The great hole in her bows, clearly visible from the shore, was only crudely patched. Much of her damaged structure was still lying about her decks. Clearly efforts had been concentrated upon refuelling and repairing vital communications in the ship.

Suddenly they heard the sounds of a muster. The crew gathered, and those who had detected the insubordinations of the previous afternoon saw no change in the attitude of the men.

The officers, who supported their Captain in his protest against the instruction to scuttle the ship, appealed for volunteers to go out and fight.

Only about sixty of the crew of 900 stepped forward. The rest had not changed their attitude. They had had enough of blood and fighting.

Just before midday there were signs of intense but unexpected activity.

At noon the *Tacoma* went alongside and heavy repair machinery—forges, welding plant, cylinders of oxygen, which had been brought from Buenos Aires—were transferred to the supply ship. Engineers and their working parties followed, and then men were seen transferring life belts. Soon none but the crew was left on the ship.

Suddenly the thousands on the Prado and the adjoining wharves were perplexed by the appearance of a launch alongside into which were shipped what appeared from a distance to be members of the crew who had suffered minor injuries.

The shrewd observers were immediately suspicious. The raider had been in harbour for two days. One of her first duties had been to bring her dead ashore and to tranship to hospital her more gravely injured. Why then were these minor casualties, who could not suddenly have required medical attention not available on board, being brought off? It was a strange development, the significance of which the many observers who had experience of sea practice, did not fail to comment upon.

Their speculations were soon communicated to the masses who were sensitive to every shade of expectation. The tragic background of the approaching drama still held the crowd, but the volatile Latin temperament could not be completely prevented from bubbling up in bursts of excited chatter and eloquent gesture.

Every fresh move, and many that were imagined, was seized upon and dissected by countless groups in the massed thousands. The pros and cons were tossed to and fro and argued over as if they were market merchandise.

There was a surge to the quayside as the launch hooked on to the steps. The men aboard were members of the raider's crew suffering from minor injuries, but there was none among the twenty-six cases that seemed to require this sudden transference to hospital ashore.

The next excitement in the damp afternoon was the disconnection of the oil pipes from the *Graf Spee*. The *Tacoma* prepared to leave. She cast off her moorings and dropped astern of the raider.

The noise of the work parties on the raider had ceased. There was still activity aboard her, but it was silent, purposeful activity. The decks were cleared, but the men began to take their sea-going stations. There were officers on the bridge. They were approaching zero hour and there was still no clear conception in the minds of the crowd as to the decision of the *Graf Spee's* Captain.

Suddenly a belch of black smoke from the raider's funnel transformed the crowd. Many had stood for hours, but weary in limb and exhausted in conversation they now threw aside their lethargy. The atmosphere was charged with the rapidly changing emotions of the crowd.

Steam up? Then she was going to sea.

There was a period of expectancy in which the silence was too much for many of the over-wrought watchers. Many women, and even men, sobbed aloud. The crowd closed over the gaps caused by the removal of those who had been overcome by the waiting and the emotional crisis.

There were still three hours to go, and the fitful rain was adding to the discomforts of the watchers ashore.

But at ten minutes past five sound was added to sight. There was a gasp and an excited roar from the crowd.

"She's weighing anchor!"

Link after link of the huge cable slowly wormed its way through the hawsepipe.

Seamen stood by with hoses playing on each link as it reached them. The fierce jets swept the mud from the cable as it jolted in link by link to the chain locker against the hum of the hoist. The anchor appeared above the water-line, its heavy flukes thick with mud and slime.

There were movements on the bridge and the attendant seamen transferred to the other side of the grey fo'c'sle. Again the crowd heard the clang as the heavy links came inboard. At twenty-five minutes past five the second anchor was up. There was a drifting cloud of black smoke from the battleship's funnel. To some it had the appearance of a pall.

In the stokehold and engine-rooms everything was being made ready for early departure.

At five minutes to six the crowd saw signalling to the *Tacoma*. Immediately she had replied, the supply ship came alongside and gangways were flung across. Numbers of the raider's crew, kit-bags on shoulders, swarmed across to the *Tacoma*.

For a quarter of an hour the stream of men seemed to be unbroken. Hundreds of them were transferred.

The crowd was at first perplexed and then almost stunned. The *Tacoma* drew away from the *Graf Spee*, and, as the gap between them increased, so consternation spread among the crowd.

Did this mean that the German captain had recognized the overwhelming odds; that he had no hope of victory? Or did it mean that he proposed to go out and fight to a finish, taking with him a few brave volunteers to work the engines and to man the guns?

"She's under way!"

The news swept through the crowd like a flame. Thousands could see little except the outline of the raider, but every word was carried to them.

The water at the stern of the German ship was churned to spume.

"She's under way! She's under way!"

The early evening was overcast; the sombre

tragedy of the scene was accentuated by the grey sky. The vast crowd was overawed.

Slowly the gaunt, grey raider moved with a silent majesty from the inner harbour. She rounded the breakwater and turned east, making for the open sea and the British cruisers that patrolled the estuary. Behind her tailed the *Tacoma* and official launches. British merchant officers and men, who had been her prisoners but were now free men, stood at the salute.

With an almost excruciating slowness the *Graf Spee* steamed along the fairway to meet her adversaries.

Suddenly she altered course. Slowly the long, lean fo'c'sle swung round and her bows pointed south-west. There was an outburst of excitement in the tense crowd. Was she returning, or was she seeking the safety of the neutral waters of Argentina in which she could legitimately claim sanctuary for a further twenty-four hours before venturing to the open sea?

At seven o'clock the *Graf Spee* stopped her engines in the middle of the estuary, just clear of the fairway and in shallow water.

She was the centre of the world's stage. Already her fate had been decided by the frenzied fanaticism of the Fuhrer in Berlin, but it had been kept secret. The world waited; it was a drama beyond the bounds of nationality. In a war that had so far resolved itself primarily in terms of naval warfare, this was the dynamic crux of a great engagement.

All other news took second place. Radio programmes were interrupted; many services gave a minute-by-minute transmission of each succeeding detail of the drama. Never in the history of radio had there been such a signal opportunity for bringing the whole world into touch with every movement of a drama as it was being enacted.

Just before half-past seven, in an overhanging gloom that robbed many of the watching thousands of a detailed view, the German commander, Captain Langsdorff, obeying direct orders from Berlin, wrote "Finis" to one of the most remarkable chapters in naval history.

As the raider lost speed and stopped, launches that had been following her came alongside. The skeleton crew that had brought the raider out of the harbour was swiftly transferred to them. The ship's officers followed them. Captain Langsdorff was the last to leave.

The waiting masses could see nothing of the Captain's departure. All that was left to them was a sight of the dull, grey mass, motionless in the vast estuary. They did not even know that the Captain had left his ship. Only those with high-power glasses could watch the departure of the launches.

Langsdorff sat in the stern sheets of the last launch, heading for Buenos Aires, with its large German colony. He had fulfilled orders from the Fuhrer; bitter orders. On his instructions he had had placed bombs with varying time fuses in all the vulnerable parts of the pocket battleship.

Suddenly the obscurity was shattered by a fierce light that illuminated the whole sky and limned the bleak outlines of the raider in a grim but unforgettable photograph.

A gasp went up from the crowd and had scarcely died away when the dull roar of an explosion reached their ears. It rolled across the heavens like thunder.

Across the miles of water thousands gazed dumbfounded.

The raider was destroyed, but by what means none at first could tell.

It might have been a torpedo. But gradually the fierceness of that sheet of flame burnt itself into the consciousness of the vast crowd. They had seen the majority of her crew leave before she put to sea. They had seen or heard that launches had taken off the remainder. There could be only one answer.

There was a numbness in the crowd as the

"*Daily Telegraph*"

With her 11-in. guns almost awash, the "Graf Spee" slowly settles.

realization dawned, and as they watched the great ship burning fiercely, the tragedy of her ignoble end became more cruelly apparent.

The dense smoke from the explosions hung like a pall over the stricken ship. From time to time there were further shattering detonations as another bomb exploded or the flames reached a magazine. Each flash revealed her gaunt outlines. The control-towers and the funnel were still visible, but much of her superstructure had been blown away.

The pride of the German Navy, the alleged invincible, had perished by the hand that created her. Her armaments were speechless, her scientific secrets were of no avail. The loyalty that had been bestowed upon her was no longer allowed to serve.

The waters seethed about her. The smoke pall seemed to mingle with the heavy clouds above her, as though to hide her shame.

Aeroplanes circled overhead. H.M.S. *Cumberland*, which had returned from the Falklands after taking the German prisoners from the *Ajax*, now appeared and from the fringe of neutral waters threw the stark glare of her searchlights upon the sombre scene.

All through the night the crowd stood fast. Dense banks of heavy smoke hung about the wreck. A dull glow illumined the clouds above.

There was no flame now, no explosions, only the melancholy aftermath as the raider slowly settled in the shallow water of the Plate. There was mercy in the curtains of the night.

Dawn brought disillusionment. Drama there had been, but no fight. The tens of thousands turned their backs and resumed their daily avocations. An official German News Agency announcement stated that "the Fuhrer and supreme commander gave the order to Captain Langsdorff to destroy the ship by blowing it up, inasmuch as the Uruguayan Government declined to allow the time necessary to make the ship seaworthy." The statement had the hollowness of unrelieved defeat.

Aboard the British cruisers ceaselessly patrolling the estuary no vigilance was relaxed but loud speakers brought to every deck the minute-by-minute story of the drama as it was enacted. But though robbed of victory in the fight, danger was still about them. The food ships would sail with greater freedom now that the raider had gone, but the rigours of patrol were unceasing. The British squadron must be about its business, after a brief respite for its harassed crews.

Captain Langsdorff looked back at the wreckage of his ship.

The man who had hastened to pay tribute to the "inconceivable audacity and incredible manœuvres" of his British adversaries, realized more than anyone that the orders he had received would leave an indelible blot upon the traditions of the sea, which Imperial Germany, at least, had often enhanced.

He was worn and broken when he stepped ashore at Buenos Aires.

"I have saved my men," was all he would say. All he desired was rest and solitude.

It had been no secret to intimates that from the first moment of the decision which had been contrary to all his instincts, Captain Langsdorff had made up his mind to share the fate of his magnificent ship.

He had not disguised his revulsion from the orders shouted from Berlin. There was but one way out with honour.

After spending several hours with his brother officers on the Tuesday evening he retired to his room and gave orders that he was not to be disturbed.

The next morning he was found dead by his own hand. His body was covered with the flag of Imperial Germany.

Meantime Montevideo, which city was already caring for many of those wounded in the Battle of the Plate, left no doubt as to where their sympathies lay. The Uruguayan Chamber of Deputies, with an unusual unanimity, voted its unqualified approval of all that the Government had done in the matter of the *Graf Spee*. The German threats had passed them by. Now they were anxious to have opportunity of doing honour to the victors.

With a swiftness that was reminiscent of the immediate reward of valour in Elizabethan days, His Majesty the King signalized the completion of this fine naval victory by causing the following announcement to be made:

"In recognition of the gallant successful action fought by H.M. Ships *Ajax*, *Achilles* and *Exeter* against the German battleship *Graf von Spee*, His Majesty the King has been pleased to appoint Commodore Henry Harwood to be a Knight Commander of the Most Honourable Order of the Bath; and Captains W. E. Parry (H.M.S. *Achilles*), C. H. L. Woodhouse (H.M.S. *Ajax*) and F. S. Bell (H.M.S. *Exeter*) to be Companions of the same Order.

"Commodore Harwood has also been promoted to be a Rear-Admiral in H.M. Fleet, to date from December 13, the date of the action.

"The Admiralty have called for recommendations from Rear-Admiral Harwood in respect of the good conduct and forwardness in action of the officers and men in the squadron under his command."

So Montevideo was already aware that she would entertain Rear-Admiral Harwood and his gallant officers and crews. Sir Henry had already asked permission to enter Uruguayan waters and had been accorded not the regulation twenty-four hours, but forty-eight hours, which the Uruguayans strove to fill with every form of acclamation.

As H.M.S. *Ajax*, flying the flag of the Rear-Admiral, and commanded by Captain Woodhouse, steamed slowly up to the inner harbour she passed the wreck of the *Graf Spee*, passed the *Tacoma* which was now interned, and received a victor's welcome from a huge crowd as she berthed.

President Baldomir received Sir Henry Harwood, and later, at one of the many festivities arranged for the victors by official organizations and prominent citizens, Dr. Serrato, a former President, said: "Men of the British Navy live, fight and die, if necessary, to defend the rule of right, so that democratic peoples and our own descendants may live free in the land of their birth."

Sir Esmond Ovey, K.C.M.G., British Ambassador to the Argentine Republic, flew from Buenos Aires to Montevideo to congratulate Sir Henry Harwood. He brought with him a cheque for £1,000 from the British community in Argentina for distribution among the dependants of those killed in the Battle of the Plate.

H.M.S. *Achilles*, showing little damage from the fierce fight, received permission from the Argentine Government for a stay of forty-eight hours to refuel and revictual. She was met at Buenos Aires by the British Ambassador and the staff of the Embassy, and her Captain, officers and crew were feted.

With the exception of Nazi Germany the whole world resounded to the praise of British victory in the Battle of the River Plate.

The *New York Herald-Tribune* crystallized the comments of millions when it said: "There will be jubilation at Admiralty Arch and in Whitehall to-day and a lot of hard explaining for Dr. Goebbels's inventive propaganda machine, as the drama of the *Graf Spee* has reached its abrupt and ignominious end.

"There is nothing heroic about scuttling one's ship when not even in the immediate presence of the enemy, and it seems hardly in the German naval tradition.

"Twenty-five years ago the original Admiral Count Spee, with odds obviously and overwhelmingly against him, fought it out to the end.

"Why the Germans made this spectacular admission of defeat while there seemed a good chance of escape is anything but clear."

The British First Lord of the Admiralty, Mr. Winston Churchill, in a broadcast talk said: "The news which has come from Montevideo has been received with thankfulness in our islands, and with unconcealed satisfaction throughout the greater part of the world.

"The *Graf Spee*, which has been for many weeks preying upon the trade of the South Atlantic, has met her doom, and throughout the vast expanse of water the peaceful shipping of all nations may for a spell at least enjoy the freedom of the seas.

"The German pocket battleship, in spite of her heavier metal and commanding range, was driven to take refuge in a neutral harbour by the three British cruisers whose names are on every lip. Once in the harbour she had the choice of submitting in the ordinary manner to internment, which would have been unfortunate for her, or of coming out to fight and going down in battle like the *Rawalpindi*, which would have been honourable to her.

"She discovered a third alternative. She came out not to fight but to sink herself in the fairway of a neutral State, from whom she had received such shelter and succour as international law prescribes.

"At that time the pocket battleship *Graf Spee* knew that the British heavy ships, *Renown* and

Ark Royal were still a thousand miles away, oiling at Rio. All that awaited her outside the harbour were the two 6-in. gun cruisers *Ajax* and *Achilles*, who had chased her in, and the 8-in. gun cruiser *Cumberland*, which had arrived to take the place of the damaged *Exeter*.

"Our own losses have not been slight. There is no harm now in stating that the *Ajax*, in which was Commodore Harwood, now, by His Majesty's pleasure, Rear-Admiral Sir Henry Harwood, K.C.B., had two of her four turrets knocked out, while the *Exeter* bore up against forty to fifty hits, many of them from shells three times the weight of those she could fire back. Three of her 8-in. guns were smashed, and she sustained nearly a hundred casualties, by far the greater part killed.

"Nevertheless the *Exeter* remained outside the harbour of Montevideo, ready, although crippled, to take part in a fresh attack, and she only departed to care for her wounded and injuries when she was relieved by the timely arrival of the *Cumberland*."

The Battle of the Plate was over, and it was, as Mr. Churchill himself was subsequently to say, a battle that would long be told in song and story.

The raider, with her perpetual menace to the freedom of the seas, had been removed. But somewhere on the high seas was living evidence of her ravages. The British crews of her victims were still in enemy hands. The lion had gone to an ignoble death, but the jackal still skulked. The stalking of the cringing jackal was soon to add another unfading leaf to the laurels of the British Navy.

CHAPTER IX

"THE NAVY IS HERE!"

WHEN, on the morning of December 7, the jackal *Altmark* was sent home by the lion *Graf Spee*, her dangers increased with each mile she drew nearer Europe. She had many problems to face, all made more acute by the presence on board of 300 British prisoners.

She adopted many ruses to escape detection. Sometimes she was the *Hangsund*, sometimes the *Chirqueue*. She carried several neutral flags.

At first she headed due south, and the prisoners could tell by the heavy seas and increasing cold that they were south of the Cape and it was not long before several of the experienced seamen agreed with each other that they could "smell ice."

For three weeks she loitered in the South Atlantic, almost on the fringe of the Antarctic Circle. During this time the *Altmark* was "playing 'possum." Her speed during this period seldom exceeded three knots. She hoped by this policy to lose contact with the world and particularly with her enquiring enemy.

The faith of the British merchantmen in the British Navy never faltered, and suddenly it received remarkable confirmation when a friendly guard surreptitiously conveyed the information that Captain Dau had had very bad news. It took some time to extract the full details, but eventually he revealed the whole truth—that the *Graf Spee* had been driven into Montevideo Harbour after fierce action with three British cruisers. She had then been scuttled on direct orders from the Fuhrer in Berlin.

Jubilation was suppressed, for fear of getting the informant into trouble, because the German captain was a martinet, but delight among the prisoners was unbounded and if any confirmation were needed of the welcome news, it came in the meals placed before them. Their monotony was now frequently relieved by the addition of luxuries, such as glacé cherries, which had obviously been intended for the officers' mess on the *Graf Spee*. For several days perishable extras were added to the prisoners' fare.

Then, without warning, the prison ship suddenly headed north. There was much speculation among the British seamen and general agreement that she must be short of fuel, although, from all appearances, she still had ample stores. Her stocks had often been replenished from the stores of the *Graf Spee's* victims.

As they approached the trade routes, look-outs were doubled and the monotony of steaming at three knots was frequently broken by bursts of speed which told the engineers aboard that she was full out.

In fact, whenever her look-outs sighted the slightest smudge of smoke it was a question of "'bout ship" and a scurry at full speed. She did, indeed, on several occasions touch 26 knots. This speed astonished the prisoners, but they had little else to relieve the monotony of their existence.

The officers had been transferred to the ammunition lockers. These were roomy and built to accommodate heavy shells. The ridges, to prevent ammunition rolling about, made the deck very uneven, but this discomfort was remedied because one of the *Graf Spee's* victims carried a cargo of coir, and this fibre was used to fill up the spaces between the ridges and thus make the deck level. Another victim carried a cargo of Persian rugs and some of these were distributed to the prisoners. They added them to their bedding.

Some of the British masters were surprised to find that their own bedding and mattresses had been transferred by the boarding parties and they were allowed to claim them. These extras made accommodation quite bearable; the chief complaint was against the absence of light and the limited opportunities for exercise on deck. The lighting problem was not of the Captain's making; such accommodation was not provided with much natural light. Whenever possible the hatch covers were removed, but even so in the short periods allowed for exercise on deck— three-quarters of an hour in the morning and half an hour in the afternoon—the men experienced much discomfort and some pain from the sudden transference to the glaring light of day.

This was particularly so when the ship reached the hotter regions, although even then there was little sustained complaint against the limited numbers allowed on deck at a time. The prisoners heavily outnumbered the crew, and the captives respected Captain Dau's capacities, also his good seamanship. It was no slight feat to have eluded not only capture but challenge in continually frequented waters.

When they refuelled at Dakar, on the West Coast of Africa, sailing under neutral colours, the Captain's plans began to be apparent to the prisoners. The sinking of the *Graf Spee* had heartened every prisoner aboard. It had increased their confidence in eventual rescue, but also underlined their fears. The *Altmark* was now not only hunted; she had lost her protector. Further, it would now be known to the British

Navy, through the *Graf Spee's* prisoners, that she was a prison ship. This worked both ways; it would increase the range of search and the Navy's prospect of success, but it would also increase Captain Dau's determination to get back to Germany as swiftly as possible.

For many days there was no lack of conversation between the British prisoners, and countless theories were argued in muttered tones as to eventual results. But, however much they differed, on one thing they all shook hands. The *Graf Spee* had been sunk, and one of Germany's finest ships was at the bottom. Their chief fears were for their shipmates held in the raider. The guard could give them no information. Indeed, he was punished for conveying the brief fact of the sinking, but it was enough to make life more bearable.

After the *Altmark* had crossed the Western Ocean without being challenged she skirted the Newfoundland cod banks where the characteristic intermittent fogs gave some of the prisoners a clue to her position.

It must have been in the Captain's mind after many weeks at sea to make straight for Germany, but despite his able seamanship he ran no risks of encountering the British Northern Patrol. Instead, he went almost due north, up the Denmark Strait which separates Iceland from

Wright & Logan

H.M.S. "COSSACK."

South Greenland. Here, the cold of January and the heavy seas made life for the captives acutely uncomfortable.

They were on the fringe of the Arctic Circle when *Altmark* turned east and headed for the northern coast of Norway.

After several days of uneventful steaming the prisoners were suddenly conscious from the general bearing of their guards and the less tense atmosphere of the ship that the ordeal was over from the Captain's point of view, and they had presumably entered neutral waters. Some of them with experience of the North Atlantic estimated accurately that they had entered Norwegian territorial waters and, in fact, the *Altmark* appeared in such waters on February 14, just north of Frohavet outside the Trondheimsfjord.

She steamed south and on the same day encountered a Norwegian naval vessel, the torpedo boat *Trygg*.

The officer in command of the *Trygg* demanded the right to inspect the *Altmark* and to this Captain Dau agreed.

Since the *Altmark* then flew the German swastika and, therefore, counted as a warship, it should, according to international regulations, have been exempt from inspection, and accordingly the senior officer of the Norwegian naval forces, felt that all he was entitled to do was to verify that the ship was all she claimed to be. This was done with the help of the *Altmark's* papers, and the Norwegian naval officer was satisfied.

The sounds of the inspection could not be hidden from the prisoners. They felt the engines cease, heard the launch come alongside, the gangway lowered, and realized that the ship was being inspected by foreign naval authorities. Whatever country they represented this was the British prisoners' chance.

Pandemonium broke out among the prisoners and never was there a better excuse for raising hell. The men had been confined for weeks; some of them had not seen much daylight for many days. They shouted, they hammered, they blew S O S signals on whistles. They smashed crockery, beat upon everything that would make a noise.

The German guards retaliated by switching off the lights, but the darkness only increased the din. Back came the Germans with fire hoses, but it takes more than water to quench the spirits of 300 British merchant seamen when release is almost within grasp. The Germans threatened them with cudgels, turned on the steam deck-winches to drown their noise, and still they were not heard.

After the withdrawal of the Norwegian party the prisoners were faced with a curt "Notice to Prisoners." It read:

"On account of to-day's behaviour of the prisoners, they will get bread and water only to-morrow, instead of the regular meals. Further, I have given an order that neither the Prisoner-Officer, nor the Doctor, will make their regular rounds after this. Any severe case of sickness can be reported on occasions of handing down the food.

"J. S. DAU, Commander.

"At sea, Feb. 15, 1940."

It is almost incomprehensible that after such happenings, the Norwegian Foreign Minister, Dr. Halvdan Koht, in the Norwegian Parliament on February 19, could say that the British "knew already what we Norwegians were unaware of, namely, that there were many British prisoners on board."

How such an infernal noise and intense physical activity could have escaped the notice of the boarding officer seems inexplicable.

The Norwegian officer was informed and noted that the ship was armed with anti-aircraft guns, but this was in accordance with the contents of the ship's papers.

However, the naval authorities in Bergen were not satisfied, and when the German prison ship reached the northern boundary of the Bergen military district, about seventy to eighty nautical miles north of Bergen, another Norwegian naval vessel arrived and demanded the right of inspection. This was on February 15, and Captain Dau refused inspection, which action was quite within his rights. The Norwegian demand was thereupon withdrawn.

After the *Altmark* had been forced to heave-to for this challenge it was discovered that she had made use of her wireless for transmission. This act is forbidden to foreigners in Norwegian waters. A caution was delivered and the German captain demanded to know the reason. When informed he stated that he had no knowledge of this ban and it appears that he then ceased to use his wireless transmitter.

The next day, February 16, the prisoners were surprised to hear aeroplane engines overhead. They could not see the visitors, but from the sounds they seemed to be hovering over the *Altmark*. They might, of course, have been Norwegian 'planes, but the British prisoners hoped against hope that they were British craft and that their prison ship had been detected. The *Altmark* was then just outside the Joessing Fjord and the aeroplanes were, in fact, British craft whose continual search over weeks had at last been rewarded.

Mr. Winston Churchill's orders had been that this ship must be found at all costs. From the moment that the British prisoners, released at Montevideo from the *Graf Spee* had informed the authorities of the existence of Captain Langsdorff's "annexe," ceaseless watch had been kept on all seas. The detailed description of the *Altmark* was circulated to every station and there was complete determination that she must not be allowed to deliver her British merchant prisoners to Germany, where they might be put to uses entirely outside the accepted codes of warfare.

The circling 'planes, whose engines the prisoners heard, met with no opposition. The German ship did not dare to fire her anti-aircraft guns in neutral waters, and, taken by surprise, she could not prevent the British observers from satisfying themselves that the ship over which they circled was indeed the *Altmark*, with, presumably, its complement of British prisoners still on board.

Immediately the news was conveyed to the British Admiralty it acted swiftly, as will be seen from this Admiralty communiqué:

"It will be remembered that the *Graf Spee* sank seven British merchant ships in the South

Atlantic before Christmas. The officers were made prisoners on board the pocket battleship and tolerably treated.

"The seamen, on the other hand, were confined in the *Altmark*, an auxiliary of the German Fleet, which according to the reports of the British prisoners liberated from the *Graf Spee*, was armed with concealed guns. Between three and four hundred British merchant seamen were held prisoners in this vessel, and upon the evidence of those of them who were transferred to the *Graf Spee* and later rescued, grievous hardships and severities were inflicted upon them.

"Since then the *Altmark* vanished from the seas, and no trace of her could be found until it appeared on the 15th that she was moving down the Norwegian coast, taking advantage of its peculiar configuration and endeavouring to convey these three or four hundred British merchant seamen captives through Norwegian territorial waters to confinement in Germany.

"Accordingly certain of H.M. ships which were conveniently disposed were set in motion and certain aircraft reconnaissances were made, as the result of which a vessel bearing the name of the *Altmark* and conforming in every respect to her description, yesterday afternoon [February 16] took refuge in the Norwegian fiord of Joessing, after having been sighted by coastal reconnaissance aircraft and intercepted by H.M.S. *Intrepid*, Commander R. C. Gordon, Royal Navy.

"Orders were given by the Admiralty, with the full authority of H.M. Government, to enter neutral waters, search the *Altmark*, and rescue any prisoners if found on board.

"Joessing Fiord has a dead end, and two Norwegian gunboats appeared at its mouth. The British Commander, Captain P. L. Vian, H.M.S. Cossack, was instructed to offer to place a joint British and Norwegian guard upon the ship, and to escort it with British and Norwegian warships to Bergen, where the search could be conducted and the whole matter investigated according to international law. This offer was not accepted.

"The Captain of the Norwegian gunboat stated that the ship was unarmed, that he knew nothing about any prisoners on board, that she had been examined at Bergen the day before, and had received permission to use Norwegian territorial waters on her passage to Germany."

Upon these assurances the British destroyer withdrew from territorial waters and I can well imagine the feelings of Captain Vian.

Doubtless he would have liked to have taken

the law into his own hands, but in so doing he would have violated the neutrality laws. He realized that the points at issue would need all the subtleties of a legal mind to elucidate them, and he was a man of action, not words. Yet a thoughtless move on his part might involve his country in serious international disputes. No doubt he wished that these were the days when a man acted first and talked about it afterwards. Had he known he might have drawn infinite encouragement from the fact that the First Lord of the Admiralty was probably at that moment thinking on similar lines.

Soon after, the wireless operator of H.M.S. *Cossack* was sitting in the radio cabin. Headphones on, he was straining his ears for messages or news. Suddenly he caught the word "Priority" and the call sign of his ship. He seized his pencil and in a few seconds he had scribbled the code and sent a messenger along to the bridge with it.

The coding officer soon had it deciphered and handed the message to the Captain. It read:

"*Admiralty to Cossack. Get the men.*"

That was all—but it was enough. Vian knew now that the Admiralty was supporting him and he could act, and act swiftly. His responsibility for the decision had ceased; now his was the equally great responsibility of carrying out the daring adventure successfully.

As the Admiralty communiqué put it laconically:

"After dark, on receipt of the Admiralty orders, the destroyer *Cossack* with the British commander on board re-entered the fiord. The Norwegian gunboats refused co-operation in the search, but remained passive."

Captain Vian had already shown the Admiralty instruction to his First Lieutenant, Commander B. T. Turner, who immediately passed the word for a boarding party to muster.

Some of the bluejackets were already standing by with grappling irons. Swiftly orders were given and executed. Men came running on deck, strapping on their accoutrements as they ran. Silently they lined up and in a few minutes the boarding party was completely armed and at the "Ready." Fenders were hung over the side. The guns crews were at their stations, and the engine-room was warned to be prepared for sudden changes.

The Captain's invitation to the Senior Officer of the Norwegian Navy on the spot, to join him in a search of the German ship, had been declined. Captain Vian had therefore no option but to proceed alone. By this time the news had spread through the *Cossack* and there was intense excitement that some of their compatriots were imprisoned in the ship which in a few minutes they were to challenge and presumably to board.

After months of patrolling the prospect of decisive action and eventual rescue was a tonic to the crew.

It was now nearing midnight and the *Cossack* swept the fjord with her searchlights. Yes, there under the lee of the shore lay the *Altmark*. She shone like silver in the fierce light. To the British captain she seemed too close inshore. The German ship had run aground, driven in some measure by the huge blocks of floating ice with which the fjord was filled. Her engineers were making superhuman efforts to free her, for they saw that without freedom of movement she would fall easy prey to the oncoming *Cossack*.

The *Cossack* had now to negotiate the channel of the fjord. Crash through the ice she went, searchlights glaring.

At that moment the *Altmark* partially freed herself and her captain began to work her engines. Her bow swung round, and for a critical moment it seemed as if the oncoming *Cossack* would impale herself upon it.

The British captain caused the helm to be

put hard over and cleared the menacing bow by brilliant seamanship in a narrow and almost uncharted channel. He brought his fo'c'sle almost alongside the *Altmark*. So close were they that Lieut.-Commander Turner saw his chance and, with revolver at the ready, leapt from the for'ard gun-mounting across the eight feet of intervening space and landed on the deck of the enemy ship.

His yell of: "Follow me, lads!" was answered with a rousing shout.

The fenders creaked. For a moment the ships separated and then came closely together again. The grappling irons were thrown over, the lines made fast, and the boarding party leaped to follow "Jimmy the One." This was indeed an engagement after their own heart, an opportunity that seldom comes to the British Navy in these days of distant engagements and impersonal warfare. It was a man-to-man engagement, reminiscent of Elizabethan days.

As soon as they landed on the deck of the German Auxiliary Ship the British seamen met with instant but feeble opposition. More than one useful boxer in the British ranks got in a dose of punishment that brought more satisfaction than all the practice bouts. The German crew were not armed and some offered physical opposition, but it was speedily overcome.

Lieut.-Commander Turner ran for'ard to the bridge, followed by the bos'n and an A.B. He was met by Captain Dau, who demanded in no uncertain terms what was the reason for this intrusion of armed force.

Then Turner asked whether the Captain held any British prisoners.

Dau, after some prevarication, agreed that he had on board about three hundred merchant officers and men.

The British naval commander then demanded to know where they were. Meantime the British boarding party had been told to search the ship and report.

A group of them, discovering a hatch cover that had been recently used, opened it up and shouted down into the obscurity: "Any Britishers here?"

There was an instant yell of "Yes!"

"Well, the British Navy's here!" was the heartening reply.

Immediately there was a wild scramble and the first of the British captives appeared over the coaming. He turned to shout to his companions: "It's all right, boys. It's true. It is the British Navy."

When the glad news spread there was intense relief and almost overwhelming excitement. For many days the prisoners had buoyed up their hopes of rescue, reinforced their faith in the British Navy, but there had been the constantly lurking fear that they might now be doomed to be taken captive to Berlin.

When the Norwegian examining officers had failed to detect their presence, or at least to acknowledge it, they had momentarily lost hope. Now the darkest fears had been dispersed by the glad sunshine of release. Cheer after cheer rang out as the prisoners swarmed round the rescue party.

While the captives were being released a number of the German crew escaped over the stern of the ship and, making their way across the ice, "reached an eminence on the shore from which they opened fire with rifles.

"The fire was returned by the British, and two Germans, who were scrambling across the ice to join those already ashore, were hit. At the same time another German fell into the water amid the broken ice. Two of the *Cossack's* officers plunged overboard and saved him."

Artificial respiration was tried for some time, without success, but in such conditions the rescue was an heroic gesture.

Some of the *Altmark's* prisoners stated that time bombs had been placed by the *Altmark's* crew in various parts of the ship, to explode at twelve-thirty, but the swift work of the boarding party saved them. If such were the case it was a fiendish thing to do, for the crew of the German tanker could have escaped over the frozen fjord, leaving the prisoners to perish.

The German captain's orders, British prisoners gathered from a seaman, were to get to Germany with his captives, or to scuttle his ship. There is no doubt that the British prisoners were intended to be used for propaganda purposes; proof, no doubt sorely needed, that the German Navy had swept Britain from the seas.

Instead, the German captain and his crew were left to meditate upon the grounded tanker. Nearby was the burnt-out shell of the German tanker *Baldur*, which, passing by outside territorial waters, was summoned to stop by the destroyer *Ivanhoe*, Commander R. H. Hadow and, as the Admiralty records, "thereupon scuttled herself in German fashion." The *Ivanhoe* rescued her crew.

No sooner were all the prisoners from the *Altmark* aboard the *Cossack* than Captain Vian was able to translate into action their longing to be home.

The British ships returned in company. Once patrol 'planes signalled drifting mines and the escorting destroyers went ahead and exploded them by machine-gun fire.

H.M.S. *Cossack* arrived at Leith on Saturday, February 17, where rescued and rescuers received a triumphant welcome. The safe arrival of the *Cossack* was a fitting conclusion to a brilliant exploit, daringly planned and as daringly executed with fine seamanship. The British public was quick to recognize this achievement, plucked as it were from the days of Drake, as a heartening reminder to the world of the fact, never in doubt in their minds, that Britain did indeed still rule the waves.

At this time Norway was a neutral under duress, whose sympathies were clearly with the Allies. Soon after the dastardly invasion of Norway by Germany on April 9, which made Norway our Ally, the award of the Distinguished Service Order to Captain P. L. Vian and Lieut.-Commander B. T. Turner, was announced.

The honours in full are printed in the appendix *pp.* 249-51.

CHAPTER X

"HOME IS THE SAILOR . . ."

THE conception and accomplishment of the *Altmark* rescue were so swift that the public were taken completely by surprise. The loitering of the prison ship in the southern waters had at least caused it to pass out of the minds of the masses, if not out of the calculations of the British Navy.

The first reactions to H.M.S. *Cossack's* brilliant feat were spontaneous but differed little from the eventual considered judgment. "Nice work!" "Good old Winston." "About time the neutrals woke up from their dreams."

Such were the comments heard in the crowd, and when the general public savoured the exploit in its full detail, they found it good. Here, indeed, was a feat that brought a splash of fine colour to the drab canvas of war. The rescue was reminiscent of Stevenson's romances, and there was a touch of Captain Kettle about it, to which a seafaring nation always responds.

It was unlikely that the Navy would allow the jackal to escape. For weeks she had eluded the British ships, with luck and guile but also with a cleverness that the searchers would be the first to accord to her Captain's credit. But the Navy would have been bitterly disappointed if their unrelenting search in many waters had been in vain. They could not, however, count on the opportunity for such a brilliant "kill." A dramatist could scarcely have conceived a more rousing ending to what will become a naval epic.

The First Lord of the Admiralty signalled to Captain Vian in H.M.S. *Cossack*:

"The force under your orders is to be congratulated on having in a single day achieved a double rescue, Britons from captivity and Germans from drowning."

That message crystallized the feelings of the people. With the subsequent diplomatic and international exchanges they had little patience. The aim and the spirit of the enterprise were unquestionable. With the living spirit personified in this rescue, they had little patience with technical niceties. The man in the street saw clearly that international law had been flagrantly violated by the German ship, whose Captain proposed, no doubt, to demand even further violation of its rules by the acceptance and transport of the British prisoners through Norway to Germany. The British forces had done all they could to secure active Norwegian co-operation in their request for a search.

The German captain in neutral waters should have released the prisoners. Failing that the Norwegian authorities who, with the rest of the world, must have known that the *Altmark* was a prison ship, should surely have given the ship not a perfunctory but a thorough search. The Norwegian authorities should have discovered the prisoners and, having done so, enforced their release.

The British authorities exhausted every means in their power to secure the enforcement of the law before taking it in their own hands. Their action, which coincided throughout with the dictates of humanity, was a technical offence in that it involved attacking a belligerent ship in neutral waters. But the Germans, with no excuse on their side, had violated neutral waters in order to break the law. The British rescue party entered neutral waters with every provocation and after exhausting every possible alternative, in order to thwart that illegal manœuvre.

Once again the British public, which on principle generally differs with its politicians, found itself in complete agreement with the Government's statement of the position. The communication to the Norwegian Government read:

"It was notorious that the *Altmark* had

H.M.S. "Cossack" prepares to board the stranded "Altmark" in Joessing Fjord, Norway

participated in depredations of the *Graf Spee*, to which she had been acting as an auxiliary.

"We had the best of reasons, confirmed by the British subjects taken off the *Graf Spee*, and previously imprisoned in the *Altmark*, for knowing that there were some 300 or 400 British subjects aboard who had for long been living under intolerable conditions.

"The *Altmark* was also credibly believed to possess offensive armaments.

"The record of this ship must have been well known to the Norwegian Government, and in the view of H.M. Government it was incumbent on the Norwegian authorities when she entered Bergen and requested passage through Norwegian territorial waters to subject her to a most careful search.

"His Majesty's Government would be grateful for full particulars as to how this search was conducted and what facts were discovered.

"Reports received by His Majesty's Government indicated that the examination had been perfunctory, as shown by the fact that no prisoners had been discovered.

"So far as the facts were at present known to His Majesty's Government it appeared to them that the Norwegian Government had failed in their duty as neutrals.

"If they had in fact found British prisoners on

board, what would they have done with them? Either they would have released them or would at any rate have held them pending full examination of the position.

"His Majesty's Government felt therefore that they had every right to complain of the inaction of the Norwegian Government.

"As stated above, 300 British had been kept for weeks and months in close confinement, and if these prisoners had found their way to a camp in Germany the Norwegian Government would have been responsible for the fate of these men.

"Meanwhile the case against the ship itself was such that His Majesty's Government were justified in pressing that the *Altmark* should be interned."

Britain had said her last word, the men were back home again, some, within a day or two, back on the high seas again. Britain turned to the now doubly acceptable pleasure of welcoming home the victors.

Ajax had slipped into home waters secretly some days before. War conditions did not permit her arrival to be announced. But the warmth of her welcome had been none the less stirring.

Then, on Thursday morning Plymouth awoke to find that *Exeter*, under cover of darkness, had slipped into Plymouth Sound. At dawn she was revealed at anchor about a mile from the Hoe. Now *Exeter* and her gallant sister ship *Ajax* lay safely in home waters, and for *Exeter* Plymouth meant more than mere home waters, it meant the home county, the home port for so many of her men.

The news spread with the gathering light. Crowds swarmed to every vantage-point. The cheers of welcome went out to meet the ship as she made her victor's way up the harbour. At many stages she was quite close to the shore which was packed with people. They saw her damaged masts, her splinter-riddled funnels. But they also saw and heard the cheering men.

At Devil's Point, where the cruiser swung round to enter the harbour, Royal Marines paraded and cheered. The cheers were returned by the crew who now lined the decks. The ship's band of Royal Marines played the *Exeter's* own song: "We are the *Exeter*, straight from the West."

As she passed Mount Wise, headquarters of the Commander-in-Chief, the First Lord of the Admiralty, Mr. Winston Churchill, was there to take the salute. He was accompanied by the Chancellor of the Exchequer, Sir John Simon, Sir Dudley Pound, First Sea Lord, and Sir Martin Dunbar-Nasmith, V.C., Commander-in-Chief of the Western Approaches.

The British cruiser was followed on the last stages of her journey by a launch wearing the Admiralty flag, and soon after the cruiser berthed she was boarded by Mr. Churchill and others.

Mr. Churchill, of all our men of action probably the most feared by the enemy but the most respected and admired by those who serve him, addressed the ship's company informally gathered to meet him.

He said:

"In this sombre dark winter, when, apart from the Navy, we have been at war and yet not at war; in these long winter months, when we have had to watch the agony of Poland and now of Finland, the brilliant action of the Plate, in which you played a memorable part, came like a flash of light and colour on the scene, carrying with it an encouragement to all who are fighting—to ourselves and to our Allies; and carrying with it the cause of rejoicing to free men and to free people all over the world. You cannot but recognize that you had the fortune to be on the spot when the opportunity came.

"All over the world, as you know, your comrades in the Royal Navy are ardently and eagerly awaiting for an opportunity to emulate your example. Here at Plymouth, where our flotillas guard the western approaches and where, under Admiral Nasmith's direction, such notable successes have been attained in the war against the U-boats, here we are specially able to congratulate you upon the fortune which enabled you to fight an action in the old style, instead of a long and intricate struggle with the mines and the U-boats which our comrades in the flotillas have been waging here.

"This great action will long be told in song and story. When you came up the river this morning, when you entered the harbour and saw the crowds cheering on the banks, one may almost think that there were other spectators in the great shades of the past, carrying us back to the days of Drake and Raleigh, to the great sea dogs of the olden times. If their spirits brooded on this scene you would be able to say to them: 'We, your descendants, still make war and have not forgotten the lessons you taught.'

"Many months, perhaps some years, of anxious struggle lie before us, and we face the future in a spirit of serious resolve. You have all lost good comrades and shipmates who are not here with us to-day, but you are here, and your gallant ship is back to cheer the hearts of your fellow-countrymen; and you have come back with the firm knowledge of having worked notably, and faithfully accomplished in a worthy cause, with your honours gathered and with your duty done.'

Later Mr. Churchill visited H.M.S. *Ajax* and told the men: "You are going to see the King."

Then Plymouth gave itself up to acclaiming the victors. Swiftly a civic welcome was announced for the next day. Earlier intimation of *Exeter's* arrival had been impossible, but Plymouth was determined that the short notice should in no way handicap their efforts.

Shock troops of the catering world swarmed over the Guildhall rooms. The Food Controller's offices and staff made hasty but willing retreat. The Guildhall was transformed into a magnificently attired banqueting-hall.

There, next day, after a triumphal march through the streets, the men of *Ajax* and *Exeter* gathered as guests of the city and its Lord Mayor, Lord Astor. The bells of St. Andrew's Church had rung out to greet them as they had rung for the triumphs of Drake and Nelson.

"It's a strange thing—this spirit of the Navy," Lord Astor said. "It is invisible, intangible, and imponderable, and now we know its audacity is incredible. It is not guns, nor is it armour, and it is not Fleet Orders. It is something which is nursed and nourished and is found where men live close together in hourly and daily danger all their lives."

"I only wish," said Captain Bell of the *Exeter*, "I had been able to bring back all my men.

Some were left behind, but I would like to tell those they have left that their husbands and their sons died gloriously, and if it had not been for them we might not have been here now."

In the centre of the Guildhall banqueting-room was the famous Drake's Drum, which is kept at Buckland Abbey, once the home of Drake. Drake took the drum with him on his famous voyages from Plymouth, during some of which he watered his ships in the River Plate. Legend has it that the drum is heard beating when Britain is in grave danger. No one heard it beating at that joyous luncheon.

The same spirit of camaraderie was apparent at the Victory Dance in the evening. They sang the "*Graf Spee* Song."

The Captain's name was Bell,
He blew her back to . . . well, well, well . . .
If you meet old Hitler face to face,
Just tell him this from me,
That we're the boys who sank the ship *Graf
Spee.*

They larked and they enjoyed themselves and unconsciously revealed the comradeship and unity which had contributed so much to the perfect team-work in action.

In an "Excuse Me!" dance, with an audacity

that amused the officer and delighted the company, a rating "stole" Lady Astor, the Lady Mayoress, who was dancing with Captain Bell. The trivial human incident was symbolic of the splendid relations existing in the ships.

Shore leave, long leaves and their moving reunions made the next few days memorable for the victors, but the nation as well as loved ones and fellow citizens, wished to give its honour to the victors of the Battle of the Plate.

"You are going to see the King," Mr. Winston Churchill had promised, and the Navy knows the First Lord does not make promises that are not fulfilled.

On Thursday, February 22, officers and men from *Ajax* and *Exeter* began to gather in London. With them came relatives, some of whom were to receive honours posthumously awarded.

The next morning nearly 800 officers and men of *Ajax* and *Exeter* assembled at Waterloo Station and with the Royal Marines Divisional Band from Chatham and their own ships' bands, marched to the Horse Guards Parade.

The crowds were dense, but there was a special enclosure for relatives of those who had lost their lives in the Battle of the Plate.

Members of the Cabinet and of the Board of Admiralty took up their positions before the hollow square of assembled men. They were then joined by H.M. The King, in his uniform of Admiral of the Fleet, the Duke of Kent, in the uniform of a Rear-Admiral. They were accompanied by the Prime Minister, Mr. Neville Chamberlain, Mr. Winston Churchill, and Admiral of the Fleet Sir Dudley Pound, First Sea Lord.

The welcome was tumultuous. The assembled men, and indeed the crowd, had not forgotten the King's own naval service and his personal experience of action at sea in the Great War.

From a window overlooking the Parade, the Queen watched the moving scene.

After the National Anthem, the First Lord of the Admiralty presented Captain C. H. L. Woodhouse, *Ajax*, and Captain F. S. Bell, *Exeter*, to the King, who then inspected the ships' companies. The cheering was unceasing.

The Investiture followed. From a blue-covered table the King took the orders and medals and decorated each officer and man as he stepped forward. [The battle honours in full are printed in the Appendix, page 225.]

Among those who received honours was the widow of Marine W. A. Russell, H.M.S. *Exeter*, who had his left forearm blown off and his right arm shattered and yet refused all but primary aid. He spent his time cheering on his shipmates and such was his spirit that it was hoped that he would survive even the dangers of such heroic disregard of his own safety. But he died of wounds, and the King conferred upon his widow the Conspicuous Gallantry Medal, and expressed his sympathy and his admiration of her husband's magnificent conduct.

After these moving moments, with which the crowd had associated itself by a sympathetic silence, the roar of triumph again ascended as it was seen that H.M. the Queen was joining the King. Together, and attended by Mr. Chamberlain and Mr. Churchill, they mounted the saluting base for the March Past.

From the Horse Guards Parade the procession emerged to receive, not without an endearing modesty and amused perplexity, the full-throated welcome of London and of the Empire of which London is still the living centre.

Meantime, with the air alive with cheering, the King and Queen walked over to where the relatives of those who had fallen were gathered. With complete informality and with that shining sincerity which has done so much to endear the King and Queen to their people, they talked with the widows and mothers, understanding their anguish, knowing the heartbreak of children left fatherless. They were a man and woman united in sympathy with those who suffered in a common cause. It was a moment that added lustre to the Navy's victory.

The capital was now taking up the welcome. All along the Embankment the crowds packed. Shipping sounded its sirens, women ran out and embraced the men. There were cheers for the Captains, cheers for the Fleet Air Arm's representatives, cheers for all and everyone as the procession smiled along to the Guildhall.

There the Lord Mayor and the City Fathers were assembled to greet the victors. The great hall which had accorded welcomes to rulers of many lands, now welcomed the officers and men who had added the Battle of the Plate to the annals of the British Navy. Britain and the British Empire could do no more. This was the seal of gratitude upon an historic occasion.

The doors of the Guildhall closed. The crowd outside still cheered.

Inside the historic hall the pageantry began to take shape. The colours shifted and merged; with a friendly orderliness the pattern was revealed. It was a pattern that will take its place in the fine tapestry of Britain's history.

CHAPTER XI

THE EMPIRE'S WELCOME

ON Friday, February 23, when the heart of the Empire was welcoming officers and men of H.M.S. *Exeter* and H.M.S. *Ajax*, the third cruiser of that splendid trio was receiving a triumphant welcome in New Zealand. It was a home-coming for her because the cruiser had been lent to the New Zealand Government and for some years before the outbreak of war had been the chief representative of the King's Navy in New Zealand waters.

In September, 1939, *Achilles* was one of the first fruits of Empire offering to the Home country in her trial. Manned by hundreds of New Zealand men, she joined the South American Division of the West Indies Station.

Now she steamed home victoriously, commanded by Captain W. E. Parry, whose brilliant tactical manœuvring had brought his ship practically unscathed through the fierce Battle of the Plate.

There must have been in many minds a recollection of the return of H.M.A.S. *Sydney* after she had sunk the German raider *Emden* at the Cocos Islands in the Great War.

A swarm of small craft waited for *Achilles* at the heads of Auckland's fine harbour. Every whistle and siren was sounded. The rash of small islands in the approaches was crowded with happy throngs.

When the British cruiser, with no visible signs of her fight, slowly berthed, the Governor-General, Lord Galway, went aboard and conveyed the nation's welcome to the ship's company.

A crowd estimated at 100,000 welcomed the victors as they marched through the flag-decked streets to the Town Hall. At the Civic luncheon the Deputy Prime Minister, Mr. Fraser, read telegrams from the British and Australian Governments joining in the welcome, and the French Consul conveyed the congratulations of the French Minister of Marine.

Mr. Anthony Eden, Secretary of State for Dominion Affairs, on behalf of the United Kingdom Government sent greeting in these terms:

"His Majesty's Government in the United Kingdom have learnt with great pleasure of the arrival in New Zealand of H.M.S. *Achilles* fresh from the great battle which led to the destruction of the *Admiral Graf Spee*. The heroic and skilful part which she played in that notable victory will long be remembered in the annals of naval history and has added lustre to the record of New Zealand's achievements in the struggle for liberty and justice in which we are engaged. New Zealand may well be proud of her sons who have given such signal proof of the contribution which New Zealand is making towards the common victory.

"We feel it particularly appropriate that H.M.S. *Achilles* should arrive home in New Zealand on the day on which the officers and men of H.M.S. *Ajax* and H.M.S. *Exeter* are being reviewed by his Majesty the King. We should have been happy if it had been possible for the officers and men of H.M.S. *Achilles* to be similarly honoured in London at the same time, and although circumstances have not rendered this feasible we can assure them that the gallant part which they took in the action will be present to the minds of all here.

"To all the officers and men of H.M.S. *Achilles* his Majesty's Government in the United Kingdom send warmest greetings and best wishes for their future welfare and success."

In acknowledgment the New Zealand Government associated themselves with every aspect of the welcome to the *Ajax* and *Exeter* men in London and conveyed the greetings of the officers and men of *Achilles* to their comrades in successful arms.

The greetings formed a happy feature of the Guildhall ceremony, at which every mention of *Achilles* was accorded a welcome that left no doubt of the company's appreciation of her vital part in the battle.

The 850 naval guests, filling to capacity the ancient hall, were swift to recognize the happy coincidence of celebration, satisfying in itself and also a significant demonstration of Empire unity.

The Lord Mayor of London, Sir William Coxen, read telegrams of mutual congratulation exchanged between himself and the Mayor of Auckland. Only physical distance separated the three ships and their men. In spirit they were still together.

Greetings came also from the Governor of the Falkland Islands and from the British wounded there. They were never out of the minds of the assembled company for there were eager and insistent tributes from the men present to the splendid welcome and hospitality offered by the British community and all officials when, after the battle, the British cruisers had taken their wounded and sought a little respite themselves at the Falklands.

The Lord Mayor had splendid and impressive

support in the City's welcome. He was accompanied by his Sheriffs, Aldermen and Common Councilmen of the City Lands Committee in their robes. The City Remembrancer, the Lord Mayor's sword-bearer, his chaplain, his sergeant-at-arms, carrying the mace, gave the full majesty of a great occasion.

It was fitting that the guests should include many of the British merchant captains whose ships had been sunk by the *Graf Spee* and whose prisoners they had been, some of them for months.

Mr. Winston Churchill was accompanied by members of the War Cabinet, Admiral of the Fleet Lord Chatfield, Sir Kingsley Wood, Sir Samuel Hoare and Lord Hankey. Mr. Anthony Eden, the Dominions Secretary and Admiral of the Fleet Sir Dudley Pound, First Sea Lord and Chief of Naval Staff were present.

There were thunderous cheers as Captain Woodhouse took his seat at the Lord Mayor's right hand, with Mr. Churchill next to him, and Captain Bell on the Lord Mayor's left.

Every member of the ships' companies had already received a souvenir from the Corporation of London in the form of a leather cigarette-case bearing the City's arms. The band of the Royal Marines, Portsmouth Division, played during luncheon.

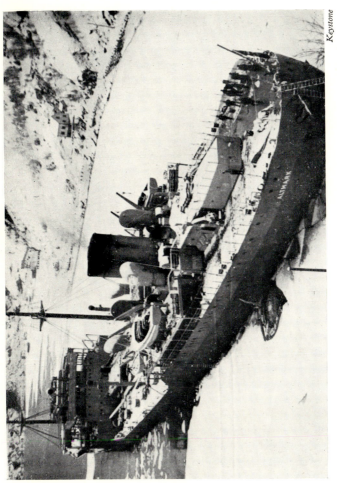

THE "ALTMARK" AFTER THE BRITISH BOARDING PARTY HAD TAKEN OFF THE BRITISH PRISONERS.

The Lord Mayor offered the toast of "The Officers and Men of H.M.S. *Ajax* and *Exeter*." He referred to the pride with which he fulfilled this duty which was a pleasure, to welcome the victors of the battle which had given the people of this country and Empire the greatest thrill since the war began. It was his regret that Rear-Admiral Sir Henry Harwood and the crew of H.M.S. *Achilles* were not present to share in this welcome in the heart of the Empire.

Captain C. H. L. Woodhouse, *Ajax*, recalled that for eighteen months before the war *Exeter* and *Ajax* had formed the South American Division of the American and West Indies Squadron. He recalled the varied activities of their service and the rescue work at the Concepcion earthquake.

Whenever the ships were at sea and whenever opportunity could be found, *Exeter* and *Ajax* carried out the numerous exercises necessary for developing their fighting efficiency. They gradually drew very close together and understood and appreciated each other very well.

The *Achilles* had been doing similar work, maintained and largely manned by the Dominion of New Zealand. They had good cause to be grateful to those who had arranged that the British forces in the South Atlantic should be strengthened early in the war by the very gallant and efficient sister-ship *Achilles*.

They felt now that their encounter with the *Graf Spee*, early in the morning of a nice fine day, and with plenty of sea room, had made them the envy of the rest of the British Navy.

Admiral Sir Henry Harwood, after three years in command of the *Exeter* and as Commodore of the South American Division, shifted his broad pennant to the *Ajax* about six months before the Battle of the Plate. Captain Woodhouse wished that he could have been present at the Guildhall and hoped that the wireless receiver which the Admiral kept in his sea cabin of his flagship was working satisfactorily at that moment.

The Commander of *Ajax* said that he spoke for every officer and man serving in his ship when he returned thanks for the tremendous welcome they had received on their return home. They intended to show their gratitude by resuming their job with even greater determination than before to see that job through so long as they might be required.

Captain F. S. Bell, responding on behalf of *Exeter*, said that none of them could possibly have imagined that as a result of what they did on that day in December they would find themselves the honoured guests of the Lord

Mayor and Corporation of the capital of the Empire.

What did they do on that Wednesday morning? Nothing very much, really, but that which every officer and man was so accustomed to do that it was second nature to him. They carried out their orders to the best of their ability. That characteristic of being able to carry out orders was, he thought, rapidly becoming inherent in their make-up, because they all realized that by exercising self-discipline the community in which they lived was benefiting as a whole. There was something perhaps more important than self-discipline, and that was training.

He felt he would be sadly lacking if he did not tell his hearers what they owed to their Commodore, Rear-Admiral Sir Henry Harwood. In peace he trained them for battle, and although the speaker did not have the honour to command the *Exeter* before the war he knew that the Commodore had worked unceasingly and untiringly for the single goal before him. When war came many monotonous days and nights were spent at sea, but they were not wasted, and training continued. Sir Henry Harwood perfected his plan with a shrewdness and far-sightedness beyond description.

Eventually the moment came when he could put his plan into action. All they had to do was to carry out his very clear and lucid instructions, and that they did to the very best of their ability. To illustrate how clear and lucid his instructions were, not one signal was exchanged between the Admiral and the *Exeter* between the time when first contact was made with the enemy and the time when the *Exeter* fell out of the action.

The references to Sir Henry Harwood were given particularly happy point by the presence in the gallery of Lady Harwood, together with Mrs. Woodhouse and Mrs. Bell.

When the First Lord of the Admiralty, Mr. Winston Churchill, rose, the great assembly knew that a man of action would accord a fine naval occasion the eloquence it deserved.

After thanking the Lord Mayor and the City of London for the hospitality they had extended to "the brave sea captains and hardy tars who won the Battle of the River Plate," Mr. Churchill continued:

"It is an action at once joyous, memorable and unique. It is the highest compliment which your Corporation can give to the officers and men of the *Ajax* and *Exeter*, and through them to the whole of the Navy, upon whom our lives and the State depend.

"I do not suppose that the bonds which unite the British Navy to the British nation—and they have taken a long time to form—or those which join the Navy to the Mercantile Marine were ever so strong as they are to-day.

"The brunt of the war has fallen upon the sailormen and upon their comrades of the Coastal Command of the R.A.F., and we have lost nearly 3,000 lives in a hard, unrelenting struggle which goes on night and day and is going on now without a moment's respite.

"The brilliant sea-fight which Admiral Harwood conceived and which those who are here executed takes its place in our Naval annals, and I might add that, in a dark, cold winter, it warmed the cockles of the British heart.

"But it is not only in the few glittering hours, glittering, deadly hours, of action which rivet all eyes—it is not only in those hours that the strain falls upon the Navy. Far more does it fall in the weeks and months of ceaseless trial and vigilance on the stormy, icy seas, dark and foggy nights when at any moment there may leap from the waves death and destruction with a sullen roar.

"There is the task which you were discharging and which your comrades are discharging. There was the task from which, in a sense, the fierce action was almost a relief.

"It will be a comfort and encouragement to the whole Navy, to the flotillas of the Grand

Fleet, to the hunting groups, to the mine-sweepers, and to the warships and auxiliaries, now about 1,700 in number and rapidly rising—it will be a comfort to all of them that the Lord Mayor of the City of London should have wished to show so heartily approval of the way the Royal Navy is carrying on and is going to carry on, until not only the cargoes by which we live, but the high purpose we have in hand are all brought safely into port."

Mr. Churchill congratulated the First Sea Lord, Admiral of the Fleet Sir Dudley Pound, and his Deputy Chief of the Naval Staff, Vice-Admiral Phillips, for the skilful combination for which they had been responsible.

"You must remember," added Mr. Churchill, "that for one stroke that goes home—the one clutch that grips the raider—there are many that miss their mark on the broad ocean. For every success there are many disappointments. You must never forget that the dangers that are seen are only a small part of those that are warded off by care and foresight and therefore pass unnoticed.

"The Admiralty and the Fleet are learning together the special conditions of this hard and novel war, and, although mistakes and accidents will certainly occur and sorrow will fall from time to time upon us, we hope that from

Whitehall the sense of resolution and design at the centre will impart itself to all the Fleet and will lighten the burden of their task and concert the vigour of their action.

"Was it, perhaps, for instance, quite a co-incidence that had got the *Achilles* suddenly to emerge out of the vast Pacific Ocean upon the shores of far-off New Zealand in order that she should receive in the Antipodes the same warm-hearted welcome as her sister the *Ajax* and the *Exeter* were receiving in 'dear old London'?

"The spirit of all our forces serving on salt water on what to-day is, after all, a naval occasion has never been more strong than now.

"As both the captains who have spoken have said, all over the world wherever the White Ensign flies—and there are very few seas into which it has not yet penetrated—your comrades are waiting and eagerly hoping that they may have the chance which you turned to such excellent results. I am absolutely sure that I speak for the *Exeter* and the *Ajax* when I say that the most ardent wish in every heart in these ships' companies is that fortune may be kind to them and they may have another 'go at them.'

"Warriors of the past may look down, as Nelson's memorial looks down upon us now, without any feeling that the island race has lost its daring or that the examples they set in bygone centuries have faded as the generations have succeeded one another.

"To the glorious action of the Plate there has recently been added an epilogue—the rescue last week by the *Cossack* and her flotilla—under the noses of the enemy, and amid the tangles of one-sided neutrality—the rescue of British captives taken from the sunken German raider— your friend, the one you sunk.

"Their rescue at the very moment when those unhappy men were about to be delivered over to indefinite German bondage, proves that the long arm of British sea power can be stretched out, not only for foes, but also for faithful friends. And to Nelson's immortal signal of 135 years ago: 'England expects that every man will do his duty'—there may now be added last week's not less proud reply: 'The Navy is here.'"

THE HONOURS OF THE BATTLE OF THE PLATE

The London Gazette

Admiralty, Whitehall.

23rd February, 1940.

The KING having already been graciously pleased, after the first phase of the Battle, to give orders for the following appointments to the Most Honourable Order of the Bath, in recognition of the gallant and successful action with the *Admiral Graf Spee* (to be dated the 13th of December, 1939):—

To be an Additional Member of the Military Division of the Second Class, or Knights Commanders, of the said Most Honourable Order:

Rear-Admiral Henry Harwood Harwood, O.B.E., Commanding South American Division of the America and West Indies Station:

To be Additional Members of the Military Division of the Third Class, or Companions, of the said Most Honourable Order:

Captain William Edward Parry, R.N., H.M.S. *Achilles,*
Captain Charles Henry Lawrence Woodhouse, R.N., H.M.S. *Ajax,*
Captain Frederick Secker Bell, R.N., H.M.S. *Exeter;*

* Crown Coypright. Reproduced by courtesy of the Controller of H.M. Stationery Office.

An announcement to this effect was published on the 23rd of December in the Second Supplement to the London Gazette of Friday the 22nd of December, 1939.

His Majesty has now been further graciously pleased to give orders for the following appointments to the Distinguished Service Order for services in the same action:

To be Companions of the Distinguished Service Order:

Captain Douglas H. Everett, M.B.E., Royal Navy, H.M.S. *Ajax*,

Commander Douglas M. L. Neame, Royal Navy, H.M.S. *Achilles*,

Commander Robert R. Graham, Royal Navy, H.M.S. *Exeter*;
who, as Commanders of their Ships, having done all they could during the long months of waiting to perfect their Ships and Ships' companies, so that they stood the test of battle, when the day for action came, heartened all by their readiness, example and encouragement.

Lieutenant Ian Dudley De'Ath, Royal Marines, H.M.S. *Ajax*;
who, in charge of a Turret when an 11-in. shell passed through the working chamber below, went at once to the hatch, which had been blown open and was giving out sparks and smoke, to find out the damage. He gave the orders needed to ensure the safety of ammunition and at once did what he could to bring the Turret into action again. He set a fine example of courage and presence of mind.

Lieutenant Richard E. Washbourn, Royal Navy, H.M.S. *Achilles*;

who, when early in the action several splinters struck the Gun Director Tower, at once killing three men and wounding two others inside the tower, though wounded on the head by a splinter which half stunned him and killed the man behind him, continued to control the main armament with the utmost coolness. He set a magnificent example to the rest of the Director Tower crew, who all stood to their posts and made light of the incident. Thus the Primary Control kept working and secured throughout the action a high rate of hits on the enemy.

Commander (E) Charles E. Simms, Royal Navy, H.M.S. *Exeter*;

who, by his zeal and energy, brought his engines to full power in record time, and by his thorough knowledge of the ship and perfect organization, checked the damage. His calm and cheerful manner set a fine example to his fellows.

Distinguished Service Cross.

Midshipman Archibald Cameron, Royal Navy, H.M.S. *Exeter*;

who, when an 11-in. shell burst above an ammunition locker and set it alight, with great calmness and foresight ordered two guns' crews to take shelter. The locker exploded, wounding some of the second crew and setting alight another locker. As soon as the main fire abated, with the help of an Able Seaman, he smothered the flames of the burning woodwork. The two of them then threw the unexploded shells over the side. These were still hot and the brass cartridge cases were either missing or split open. The bottom row of ammunition had not burned, and this also was thrown over the side. Throughout the action he showed the utmost coolness and resource. He never failed to make the best use of his guns' crews.

Conspicuous Gallantry Medal.

William G. Gwilliam, Able Seaman, H.M.S. *Exeter*;
who helped Midshipman Cameron to smother the flames of a burning ammunition locker, and to throw hot shells, with their brass cases either missing or split open, over the side. He showed no regard for his own safety in putting out fires on the Upper Deck near the aircraft from which petrol was leaking.

Samuel John Trimble, Sergeant, Royal Marines, H.M.S. *Achilles*;
who, early in the action, when several splinters struck the Gun Director, at once killing three men and wounding two others inside the tower, was severely wounded; but stood fast without flinching or complaint throughout the hour of action that followed, bearing his wounds with great fortitude. When the medical party came he helped them to move the wounded and then made his own way to the Sick Bay with little aid.

Wilfred A. Russell, Royal Marines, H.M.S. *Exeter*;
who, having his left forearm blown away and his right arm shattered when a Turret was put out of action by a direct hit from an 11-in. shell, refused all but first-aid, remained on deck and went about cheering on his shipmates and putting courage into them by his great fortitude; and did not give in until the heat of the battle was over. He has since died of wounds.

Stoker (First Class) Patrick O'Brien, H.M.S. *Exeter*;
who, when ordered from the Damage Control Headquarters to make contact with the Main Switchboard,

found his way through the Chief Petty Officers' Flat where an 11-in. shell had just burst. Through the dense and deadly smoke, escaping steam and high explosive fumes, he made contact with the Main Switchboard and so with the Engine Room Artificer in the Forward Dynamo Room. From there he returned by way of the Upper Deck and led his party into the reeking Flat.

H.M.S. AJAX.

Distinguished Service Cross.

Lieutenant-Commander Desmond P. Dreyer, Royal Navy;
who, as Gunnery Officer of the ship, controlled the fire with great skill and ensured the high efficiency of his department.

Lieutenant Norman Kelso Tod, Royal Navy;
who carried out navigating duties with the utmost coolness and accuracy throughout the action.

Lieutenant Edgar D. G. Lewin, Royal Navy;
who was catapulted after the action had started when the air-worthiness of his aircraft was in doubt, and made a landing and recovery under difficult conditions after the battle.

Warrant Shipwright Frank Henry Thomas Panter, Royal Navy;
who, when knocked down and wounded by the explosion of an 11-in. shell which started fires, filled the compartment with smoke and put out all lights, went at once to the centre of the damage, where he encouraged and directed the repair parties and did all he could to limit and control the ill-effects.

Warrant Engineer Arthur P. Monk, Royal Navy;
  who made all preparations for catapulting the aircraft.
  He later went to the scene of the most serious damage and
  by hard and skilful work, devotion to duty and cheerful
  example, did much to keep heart in the repair parties.

Gunner Reginald C. Biggs, Royal Navy;
  who, in charge of a Turret, dealt very well with the
  failure of one ammunition hoist, and by his zeal and
  energy saw to it that his guns fired all they could in
  the time.

H.M.S. ACHILLES.

Distinguished Service Cross.

Lieutenant George G. Cowburn, Royal Navy;
  who handled the ship with the utmost skill and coolness
  and was undismayed when the Commanding Officer and
  the Chief Yeoman of Signals were wounded alongside
  him. The Ship's immunity from being hit was mainly
  due to him. The running commentary on the progress
  of the action which he passed to the Lower Conning
  Tower was of the greatest value, as it was broadcast to
  all positions between decks, including the Engine Room.

Surgeon-Lieutenant Colin G. Hunter, Royal Navy;
  who was very junior for the responsible duty of Principal Medical Officer. He is a New Zealander. He had
  gained the confidence of the ship's company and won
  their esteem and affection, and so contributed much to
  the contentment of the Lower Deck. During the
  action his first-aid organization worked very well, and
  he showed good judgment in dealing with the seriously
  wounded.

Gunner Eric J. Watts, Royal Navy;

who, though early in the action the Director Control Tower was hit by six splinters of a shell which killed or wounded half the personnel, carried out his duties as Rate Officer most ably throughout. When his rate keeping was no longer required, he left his position and calmly tended the wounded.

Gunner Harry T. Burchell, Royal Navy;

who, throughout the first action and the sixteen-hour chase which followed, carried out his duties with the greatest zeal and efficiency and relieved the Principal Control Officer of much trouble and responsibility, so that he could concentrate on observing and identifying the fall of shot. His conduct was exemplary.

H.M.S. Exeter.

Distinguished Service Cross.

Commander Charles J. Smith, Royal Navy;

who showed great calm and resource when communications had failed, in passing an order for port helm and in firing the starboard tubes at the correct moment. When required he conned the ship from aft, and after the action worked tirelessly to repair electrical damage, although wounded in the leg.

Commander Richard B. Jennings, Royal Navy;

who throughout the action controlled the main armament with great calmness and skill. When only one Turret was left in action he tried to spot from the after control position though standing over the muzzles of the guns. Throughout and after the battle he was untiring in his work of keeping the Turret in action and in directing the ship's company to clear away the debris, the Commander being wounded.

Lieutenant Aidan E. Toase, Royal Marines;
who was very active and resourceful in assisting to render the Turret safe after it had been hit by an 11-in. shell.

Surgeon-Lieutenant Roger W. G. Lancashire, Royal Navy;
who, during the action and throughout the passage to the Falklands, with no sleep, worked cheerfully and unceasingly in tending the wounded.

Midshipman Robert W. D. Don, Royal Navy;
who, throughout the action showed great calm, resource and initiative, especially in running hoses into the burning Marines' barracks, in fighting a fire over the lower steering position, and in rescuing the wounded.

Warrant Shipwright Charles E. Rendle, Royal Navy;
who controlled the shoring up and general repairs to the after section of the ship during the action. His untiring energy and great skill in effecting repairs, and so making the ship watertight after action, were beyond praise.

H.M.S. AJAX.

Distinguished Service Medal.

Albert E. Fuller, Petty Officer;
who was in charge of an electrical repair party near a compartment in which an 11-in. shell burst putting out all lights and causing much damage to electrical gear. He at once took efficient action to provide lighting and control the damage, and showed great courage, presence of mind and good leadership.

William G. Dorling, Chief Mechanician (Second Class);
who was in charge of the Stokers' Fire and Repair party
near a compartment in which an 11-in. shell burst cutting pipes and starting fires. He at once took efficient
action to control the damage and showed great courage,
presence of mind and good leadership.

Bertram Wood, Stoker (First Class);
who showed special bravery, presence of mind and forwardness in controlling damage when an 11-in. shell
burst near him. He entered "X" lobby when a number
of casualties had occurred, and, single handed, put out
a fire.

Frank E. Monk, Stoker (First Class);
who showed special presence of mind and forwardness
in controlling damage when an 11-in. shell burst near
him.

Duncan Graham, Shipwright (Third Class);
who set a magnificent example by his courage and
forwardness near severe damage.

James W. Jenkins, Electrical Artificer (Third Class);
who showed special presence of mind and forwardness in
controlling damage when an 11-in. shell burst near
him.

Raymond G. Cook, Sergeant, Royal Marines;
who showed great presence of mind and initiative in
carrying out orders when a Turret was severely hit and
fires and casualties occurred.

Thomas S. Reginald Norman Buckley, Marine;
who when a Turret was hit showed great presence of
mind and efficiency in ensuring the safety of the
ammunition.

Clarence H. Charles Gorton, Petty Officer;
who, being in charge of a Turret, worked hard and well, showed great devotion to duty, and ensured the maximum output from his Turret throughout the action.

John W. Hill, Petty Officer;
who as Director Layer, carried out his most important duties with great skill thereby contributing much to the fighting efficiency of the ship throughout the action.

Leonard C. Curd, Leading Seaman;
who carried out most important Fire Control duties, usually performed by an Officer, with marked success throughout the action, and set a fine example of cheerful efficiency.

Robert D. Macey, Able Seaman;
who, being in charge of a Shell-Room, set a fine example of cheerful and good hard work and ensured that there was no delay in ammunition supply in the Turret which was able to fire the greatest number of rounds.

Robert McClarnan, Able Seaman;
who, being in charge of a Magazine, set a fine example of cheerful, hard and skilful work.

Richard C. Perry, Stoker (First Class);
who worked with energy, skill and initiative in making repairs to the catapult motor during action.

H.M.S. ACHILLES.

Distinguished Service Medal.

Edgar V. Sherley, Able Seaman;
who was severely wounded when the Director Control Tower was hit by splinters. He behaved with great

courage during his long wait until proper medical attention came. The nearest door of the D.C.T. through which he would normally have been evacuated was jammed by splinter damage, and it was necessary to remove him by a devious and difficult route in the heat of the engagement. He gave all the help he could to the Medical Party during this painful operation. He bore the pain of his wounds with great patience and fortitude.

Ian Thomas L. Rodgers, Ordinary Seaman;
who, when early in the action several splinters struck the Gun Director Tower at once, killing three men and wounding two others inside the tower, was immediately ordered across, and proceeded to carry out essential duty coolly and skilfully for the rest of the engagement.

Allan M. Dorset, Boy (First Class);
who, though early in the action several splinters struck the Gun Director Tower at once, killing three men and wounding two others inside the tower, behaved with exemplary coolness, despite the carnage around him. He passed such information as was available to him to the guns, and repeated their reports clearly for the information of the Gunnery Officer.

William G. Boniface, Chief Petty Officer;
who, though early in the action several splinters struck the Gun Director Tower at once, killing three men and wounding two others inside the tower, maintained a good range plot throughout the engagement.

William R. Headon, Petty Officer;
who, though early in the action several splinters struck the Gun Director Tower at once, killing three men and wounding two others inside the tower, kept up an accurate output for a prolonged action of over two hundred

broadsides. He was faced with an especially difficult task in hand training with large alterations of course at full speed and with wide angles of rudder. During the lull he helped to remove dead and wounded.

Alfred Maycock, Petty Officer;
who, though early in the action several splinters struck the Gun Director Tower at once, killing three men and wounding two others inside the tower, kept an accurate output for a prolonged action of over two hundred broadsides. During the lull he helped to remove the wounded and dead.

Harry H. Gould, Able Seaman;
who, though early in the action several splinters struck the Gun Director Tower at once, killing three men and wounding two others inside the tower, maintained throughout the engagement a good range plot, even when the body of a shipmate fell on him through the D.C.T. floor.

Leslie Hood, Acting Chief Mechanician (Second Class);
who was most helpful in the Engine Room, and showed zeal and energy throughout the action.

William Job Wain, Chief Stoker;
who was, in the words of one of the staff of "A" Boiler Room, an "inspiration and help to them all." He steamed this boiler room with the highest efficiency, using great initiative in setting and adjusting the sprayers to obtain the best flame and a minimum of smoke.

Lincoln C. Martinson, Chief Yeoman of Signals;
who showed great zeal and untiring energy in training and organizing the V/S Department. The smartness of *Achilles'* flag-hoisting had been commented on both by the Commodore Commanding, New Zealand Squadron,

and the Rear Admiral Commanding, South America Division, and did not fail in battle.

When seriously wounded and in great pain, he continued to inquire after the welfare of the V/S department and wanted to know how his men were doing.

William L. Brewer, Chief Petty Officer Telegraphist;
whose training and organization of the W/T department successfully withstood the supreme test of battle. His coolness and ability, when under fire, in repairing damage to W/T equipment, on the upper deck and below decks resulted in *Achilles'* W/T being in full working order again in a very short time, and in getting the first Enemy Report through.

George H. Sampson, Chief Ordnance Artificer (First Class);
whose skilful maintenance of the gun armament material secured that at the end of the action all guns were fully in action and all hoists working. At no time was the rate of fire of any Turret slowed up by any failure in the ammunition supply or by any defect.

Albert G. Young, Cook;
whose energetic example and most cheerful demeanour were an inspiration to the rest of his quarters during the whole of this action and the sixteen hour chase that followed.

Frank T. Saunders, Sergeant, R.M.;
who acted with courage and initiative throughout the engagement, overcoming each difficulty and breakdown as it occurred, and by his fine example and leadership urged his quarters to still further efforts.

H.M.S. EXETER.

Distinguished Service Medal.

James McGarry, Engine Room Artificer (Second Class);
who on his own initiative at the beginning of the action
flooded the petrol compartment. After the two shell
bursts near him and in dense fumes, with dead and dying
around him, himself blown against a bulkhead and
temporarily stunned, he maintained complete charge.
He got Shipwrights to investigate damage and organized
stretcher parties and the work in his area. On the arrival
of the Engineer Officer he made a complete report while
a messenger supported him.

Frank L. Bond, Engine Room Artificer (Fourth Class);
who, on a shell entering the Flat in which he was, stood
fast in the dense fumes, and, waiting until the last man
was reported clear of a Magazine, then flooded it. He
then went to the main centre of the fire to ascertain
damage. He found the flooding valve spindles shot
away, the fire main shattered but enough flow of water
into the magazine from the damaged fire main. So he
carried on fighting the fire in the Chief Petty Officers'
Flat.

After the action he performed his duties with marked
zeal and cheerfulness.

Arthur B. Wilde, Sergeant, Plymouth;
who, ordering the evacuation of a Turret after the Gun
House had been hit by an 11-in. shell, calmly put a
tourniquet of rope round the stump of a Marine's arm.
He then returned to the Gun House where he found a fire
over the rammer of the left gun. This rammer contained
a charge of cordite. He organized a chain system of

238

buckets to the Turret, put out the fire, removed the cordite, and threw the charge over the side.

Herbert V. Chalkley, Acting Petty Officer;
who, shortly after an 11-in. shell burst in the Chief Petty Officers' Flat above the dynamo room in which he was, managed to open the door in the escape truck and crawl over the wreckage to the switchboard hatch. He could not clear the wreckage away, and realizing that his services could be dispensed with in the dynamo room, he scrambled up the dynamo escape trunk to the upper deck, returned to the flat and helped the fire parties in getting the fire under control and isolated circuits there. The conditions in these two flats were very bad at the time that he was trying to escape from the dynamo room. His work with the fire parties was outstanding.

Charles D. Pope, Sick Berth Chief Petty Officer;
who, when returning from the fore part of the Sick Bay with bottles of Morphine Sulphate Solution, was knocked flat and temporarily unconscious by a shell bursting and badly perforated that end of the Sick Bay. The bottles were broken, but when he recovered he went back through the smoke and fumes and not finding more solution brought back with him Morphia Ampoules.

Throughout the action he displayed great coolness, initiative and cheerful optimism despite the floods in the Sick Bay.

After the action his nursing and devotion to the wounded was exemplary.

Charles F. Hallas, Petty Officer;
who was the Torpedo Gunner's Mate in charge of the torpedo tubes. Although wounded at the start of the action he remained at his station until all torpedoes were

fired. He then formed parties to deal with fires on deck and help the wounded. After the action he worked unceasingly in repairing damaged circuits. His cheerfulness throughout was a great encouragement to all who were working with him.

John L. Minhinett, Stoker (First Class);
who, when taken wounded to the After Medical Station, refused all attention until he was certain that the message he had been carrying had been delivered. This message stated that the steering had been changed over to Number 3 position.

Eric A. Shoesmith, Acting Leading Airman, F.A.A.;
who on his own initiative, despite his clothing being soaked in petrol, climbed on to the top of the centre section of the aircraft and cleared the triatic stay which had fallen across it, thus freeing the aircraft for jettisoning. While he did this the ship was under heavy fire, the petrol leaking from the aircraft was a great danger, and a Turret was firing on a forward bearing.

George E. Smith, Plumber (Third Class);
who, shortly after the explosion in the Chief Petty Officers' Flat, took a party of Stokers there to free the Main Switchboard Room's hatch. At the time the flat was in darkness, reeking with fumes and smoke, full of debris and with the possibility of little deck supporting.

Frederick Knight, Joiner (Third Class);
who, while bleeding in the face and badly shaken by the 11-in. shells exploding on the forecastle Mess-deck, used great initiative in improvising stretchers for the wounded, in examining compartments underneath the damage and in plugging holes in the upper deck.

MR. WINSTON CHURCHILL WELCOMES THE RETURN OF H.M.S. "EXETER" AT PLYMOUTH, HER HOME PORT.

William E. Green, Petty Officer;
who, as Chief Quartermaster, when the upper steering
position was put out of action by an 11-in. shell exploding
on a Turret ensured that the secondary steering position
was correct and fully manned. Finding it to be so he
started aft to see that the after steering position also
was correct; on his way he was seriously wounded.

Joseph A. Rooskey, Chief Mechanician (Second Class);
whose work was outstanding among all those on the
catapult platforms jettisoning the aircraft. His calmness, skill and initiative were most valuable and set a
splendid example to all those around him.

Alfred J. Ball, Able Seaman;
who when taken wounded to the Fore Medical Station
himself gave first-aid to the other wounded and by his
willingness and cheerfulness was of great help to the
Fore Medical Station.

Stephen J. Smith, Petty Officer;
who was in charge of the After Repair Party. A few
minutes after the action opened a shell bursting close to
the ship aft caused the flooding of Number 3 Breaker
Room and much damage to the leads there. His
prompt action in running emergency circuits to a Turret
and the after steering motor helped to maintain the ship
in action.

Thomas G. Phillips, Engine Room Artificer (Third Class);
who got the two extra dynamos on load in record time.
As the result of an explosion he and his party were
trapped in the forward Dynamo Room which filled with
dense fumes and smoke. One dynamo had stopped and
with the exhaust fan out of action he skilfully effected
the repairs needed to get the machine running again.

Sidney A. Carter, Master-at-Arms;
> who, though wounded in the right knee and severely bruised by a splinter early in the action, carried on tirelessly and devotedly his duty in the After Medical Party.

Eric T. Dakin, Sick Berth Attendant;
> who had been in the ship only a week, having been lent from H.M.S. *Ajax*, his first ship. His conduct throughout the action was exemplary. He carried out instructions perfectly, his first-aid treatment was very good and his quiet gentle manner gave great confidence to the wounded. His ability to take charge and keep order in difficulties was splendid.

Mentions in Despatches.

H.M.S. Ajax.

Engineer Captain Lionel C. S. Noake, R.N.
Paymaster Commander Rutherford W. Moore, R.N.
Lieutenant-Commander Ralph C. Medley, R.N.
Lieutenant-Commander Richard R. S. Pennefather, R.N.
Paymaster Lieutenant-Commander Victor G. H. Weekes, R.N.
Surgeon Lieutenant-Commander Alexander J. Burden, R.N.
Lieutenant Richard E. N. Kearney, R.N.
Chief Petty Officer Henry N. Watson.
Chief Yeoman of Signals George W. Harman.
Leading Signalman Daniel F. Parrott.
Chief Petty Officer Telegraphist John F. Dagwell.
Band Corporal Angus J. H. Macdonald.
Marine Albert J. Hester, R.M.
Leading Seaman Cecil J. Williams.

Leading Seaman Henry Brennan.
Chief Ordnance Artificer (First Class) Arthur Hoile.
Leading Telegraphist Frederick J. Chatfield.

H.M.S. ACHILLES.

Commander (E) H. W. Head, R.N.
Paymaster Commander H. T. Isaac, R.N.
Lieutenant P. P. M. Green, R.N.
Lieutenant (E) Jasper A. R. Abbott, R.N.
Gunner (T) George R. Davis-Goff, R.N.
Warrant Electrician Joseph F. Swift, R.N.
Chief Petty Officer Leonard H. Boys.
Chief Petty Officer Ronald P. Burges.
Sailmaker Ivan D. Crawford.
Able Seaman Keith F. Connew.
Able Seaman James S. Borwick.
Able Seaman Collin W. Malcolm.
Able Seaman Bernard J. Sole.
Able Seaman Alexander Steve.
Able Seaman Laurence A. Webb.
Chief Engine Room Artificer (First Class) Reginald A. Martin.
Chief Stoker John W. Welham.
Stoker Petty Officer Robert M. Lobb.
Stoker (First Class) David S. Allison.
Ordinary Telegraphist Alan V. Bell.
Chief Petty Officer Cook Hubert C. Luke.
Master-at-Arms Frederick E. Loader.
Acting Corporal Leonard J. Fowler.
Marine Ray O. Osment.

H.M.S. Exeter.

Paymaster Commander Henry B. John, M.B.E.
Lieutenant Donald T. McBarnet, R.N.
Surgeon Commander John Cussen, R.N.
Sub-Lieutenant (E) John W. Mott, R.N.
Acting Sub-Lieutenant Clyde A. L. Morse, R.N.
Senior Master Ernest A. Doust, R.N.
Gunner Stanley J. Dallaway, R.N.
Stoker Petty Officer Albert S. Jones.
Chief Shipwright Anthony C. Collings.
Sergeant George W. Puddifoot.
Chief Stoker George I. Crocker.
Ordnance Artificer (First Class) William E. Johns.
Leading Telegraphist Cyril H. Lansdowne.
Electrical Artificer (First Class) Philip A. England.
Chief Petty Officer Telegraphist Harold E. Newman.
Sick Berth Petty Officer Clifford J. Scoble.
Chief Petty Officer Steward Joseph W. Watts.
Bandmaster (Second Class) Leonard C. Bagley.

APPENDIX II

LIST OF CASUALTIES
AS ISSUED BY THE ADMIRALTY

The Secretary of the Admiralty regrets to announce the following casualties sustained in action by H.M.S. *Exeter* on 13th December. Next of kin have been informed.

ADMIRALTY, S.W.1.
17th December, 1939.

KILLED

Bowman-Manifold, John	Lieutenant-Commander, R.N.
Rickcord, John Scott	Midshipman, R.N.
Tyler, Donald Howard	Paymaster Sub-Lieutenant, R.N.
Woods, Humphrey Ropner Duncan	Captain, Royal Marines

MISSING, BELIEVED KILLED

Morse, Clyde Anthony Leeds	Acting Sub-Lieutenant, R.N.

WOUNDED

Causton, Jack Edward	Probationary Temporary Paymaster Sub-Lieutenant, R.N.V.R.
Lynn, Thomas John	Acting Gunner (T), R.N.
Penn-Gaskell, Leslie de Nedham William	Paymaster Midshipman, R.N.

KILLED

Back, F. E. E.	Engine-room Artificer, 4th Class	D/MX 54889
Bethell, Frank	Able Seaman	D/JX 151055
Bethell, Joseph	Able Seaman	D/SSX 22452
Blandford, Bert	Marine	Ply/X 711

245

Bowes, R. M.	Ordinary Seaman	D/JX 150342
Bright, Daniel	Stoker Petty Officer	D/KX 78984
Burras, S. W.	Stoker, 1st Class	D/KX 92228
Campbell, F. P.	Stoker, 1st Class	D/KX 88775
Clarkson, R. M. R.	Able Seaman	D/JX 151372
Croker, A. J.	Marine	Ply/X 835
Davies, G. L.	Able Seaman	D/SSX 22679
Dove, G. H.	Acting Petty Officer	D/JX 134624
Dyer, F. W. C.	Shipwright, 3rd Class	D/MX 47145
French, F. T.	Able Seaman	D/SSX 20765
Gibson, S. C.	Able Seaman	D/JX 139907
Harrington, S. P.	Marine	Ply/22286
Harris, Hugh	Petty Officer Telegraphist	D/J 51924
Higginbottom, Alan	Chief Yeoman of Signals	D/J 100565
Hill, R. B.	Boy Bugler	Ply/X 2238
Honey, L. F.	Leading Signalman	D/JX 138212
Jones, A. S.	Stoker Petty Officer	D/K 65933
Kavanagh, M. T.	Telegraphist	D/SSX 16949
Kelly, A. E.	Stoker, 1st Class	D/KX 82448
Lumsden, A. R.	Telegraphist	D/JX 142445
Macleod, William	Stoker, 1st Class	D/KX 81482
Manning, George	Stoker, 1st Class	D/K 59242
Marsh, W. G. R.	Corporal	Ply/X 1361
McDonnell, F. H.	Able Seaman	D/SSX 15579
McEvoy, J. P.	Marine	Po/X 2091
Mill, Edward	Marine	Ply/X 1914
Monks, Christopher	Stoker, 2nd Class	D/KX 96243
Naylor, T. H.	Able Seaman	D/JX 138243
O'Leary, P. J.	Stoker, 1st Class	D/KX 92212
Parry, D. J.	Telegraphist	D/JX 141568
Pett, B. T.	Stoker, 1st Class	D/KX 92198
Pullyblank, L. W.	Leading Supply Assistant	D/MX 50647
Randall, Frank	Stoker Petty Officer	D/K 37155
Remick, Tom	Chief Yeoman of Signals	D/J 45240
Richards, Brynmoor	Able Seaman	D/JX 14118
Richards, Glyndwr	Leading Seaman	D/JX 127862
Riglar, A. S.	Telegraphist	D/JX 144826

Small, R. J.	Blacksmith, 3rd Class	D/MX 51352
Squire, E. B.	Boy, 1st Class	D/JX 158659
Steele, R. M.	Stoker Petty Officer	D/K 60833
Stubbs, Agean	Marine	Ply/X 1370
Taylor, R. W.	Telegraphist	D/JX 146419
Thompson, J. E.	Stoker, 1st Class	D/KX 81575
Tovey, G. E.	Stoker Petty Officer	D/KX 80186
Tregidgo, A. F.	Chief Petty Officer	D/J 89888
Wilson, Patrick	Stoker, 1st Class	D/KX 86441

DIED OF WOUNDS

Ainge, W. A.	Chief Petty Officer	D/J 52100
George, E. I.	Leading Stoker	D/K 65213
Hill, L. C.	Able Seaman	D/J 44825
Legg, Frank	Petty Officer Cook	D/MX 52427
Phillips, A. V.	Acting Leading Seaman	D/JX 142946
Powton, R. F.	Chief Petty Officer Cook	D/M 37983
Russell, W. A.	Marine	Ply/X 214
Spencer, Harry	Able Seaman	D/SSX 16592

MISSING, BELIEVED KILLED

Teague, S. B. P.	Chief Stoker	D/K 57454

WOUNDED

Alder, G. T. C.	Petty Officer	D/J 96447
Carroll, F. M.	Acting Leading Seaman	D/SSX 13256
Collins, A. C. P.	Chief Shipwright, 2nd Class	D/M 14336
Cunningham, James	Able Seaman	D/SSX 20333
Frederick, J. T.	Able Seaman	D/JX 143465
Glover, K. E.	Boy, 1st Class	D/JX 154501
Green, W. E.	Petty Officer	D/J 48534
Horsley, Walter	Ordinary Seaman	D/JX 151509
Lister, Andrew	Marine	Ply/X 1287
Mason, J. E. P.	Able Seaman	D/J 99351
Mellors, Albert	Leading Seaman	D/JX 134210
Roe, Arthur	Marine	Ply/X 1329
Smith, William	Stoker Petty Officer	D/KX 75905
Snowden, Cyril	Able Seaman	D/SSX 22746

Truman, W. C.	Petty Officer	D/J 86383
Tweddle, Thomas	Stoker, 2nd Class	D/KX 96174
Wallis, Stanley	Stoker, 1st Class	D/K 59471

The Secretary of the Admiralty regrets to announce the following casualties sustained in action by H.M.S. *Ajax* on 13th December, 1939. Next of kin have been informed.

KILLED

Bashford, Cyril G.	Corporal, Royal Marines	C/X 959
Burrells, Albert F. O.	Marine	C/X 1688
Clements, James H.	Marine	C/X 654
Farley, William J.	Ordinary Seaman	C/JX 151605
Follett, Harry	Sergeant, Royal Marines	C/X 688
Frankcom, Ernest A. C.	Steward	C/LX 21835
Lambard, William W.	Marine	C/X 1663

SERIOUSLY INJURED

Brown, Jack R. D.	Able Seaman	C/JX 139427
Mullard, Reginald J.	Marine	C/X 1589

Eleven other men received minor injuries only.

The Secretary of the Admiralty regrets to announce the following casualties sustained in action by H.M.S. *Achilles* on the 13th December, 1939. Next of kin have been informed.

ADMIRALTY, S.W.1.

15th December, 1939.

KILLED

Grant, I. W.	Ordinary Seaman	N.Z.D./SS 1734
Milburn, N. J.	Ordinary Telegraphist	D/SSX 23288
Shaw, A. C. H.	Able Seaman	N.Z.D./1030
Stennett, F.	Telegraphist	D/JX 148899

WOUNDED

Martinson, L. C.		N.Z.D./345
Sherley, E. V.	Able Seaman	N.Z.D./1163
Trimble, S. J.	Sergeant, R.M.	P.O./22169

THE HONOURS OF THE JOESSING FJORD INCIDENT

The London Gazette

Admiralty, Whitehall.

12th April, 1940.

The KING has been graciously pleased to give orders for the following Appointments to the Distinguished Service Order:—

To be a Companion of the Distinguished Service Order:

Captain Philip Louis Vian, Royal Navy, H.M.S. *Cossack*; for outstanding ability, determination and resource in the preliminary dispositions which led to the rescue of 300 English prisoners from the German Armed Auxiliary *Altmark*, and for daring, leadership and masterly handling of his ship in narrow waters so as to bring her alongside and board the enemy, who tried to blind him with the glare of a searchlight, worked his engine full ahead and full astern, tried to ram him and drive him ashore and so threatened the grounding and loss of *Cossack*.

Lieutenant-Commander Bradwell Talbot Turner, Royal Navy, H.M.S. *Cossack*; for daring, leadership and address in command of the party which boarded *Altmark* while the ships were manœuvring under high power, changing relative positions and not in full contact, so that he had to leap a fathom to reach her. He pulled up the Petty Officer next behind him, who had jumped short and hung by his hands, made fast the hawser, and, cheering, led his party at the double to the bridge. Having disarmed such enemy officers as carried firearms, he took over from a German first the starboard then the port telegraph and set it to "Stop" instead of "Full Speed Ahead," so that *Altmark* could not ram *Cossack*, but grounded aft on a shelf, making about 4 knots sternway.

His Majesty has also been graciously pleased to approve the following awards:—

The Distinguished Service Cross.

Paymaster Sub-Lieutenant Geoffrey Craven, Royal Naval Volunteer Reserve, H.M.S. *Cossack*;
for outstanding ability and resource as an essential member of the Boarding Party.

Mr. John James Frederick Smith, Gunner, Royal Navy, H.M.S. *Aurora*;
for prowess, leadership and devotion to duty, in command of the second section of the Boarding Party.

The Distinguished Service Medal.

Petty Officer Norman Leslie Atkins, H.M.S. *Cossack*;
for gallantry and leadership in charge of a section of the Boarding Party.
Petty Officer Herbert Tom Barnes, H.M.S. *Aurora*;
Able Seaman Peter John Beach, H.M.S. *Cossack*;
Able Seaman James Harper, H.M.S. *Cossack*;

Able Seaman Albert William Marshall, H.M.S. *Cossack*;

Able Seaman Stanley Douglas Bennett, H.M.S. *Aurora*;

Signalman Donald Phillip Samuel Davies, H.M.S. *Afridi* (Lent *Cossack*);

Stoker First Class Norman Leslie Pratt, H.M.S. *Aurora*;
for gallantry and devotion to duty in the boarding of *Altmark*.

Mentions in Despatches.

Lieutenant-Commander Hector Charles Donald MacLean, Royal Navy, H.M.S. *Cossack*;
for outstanding ability and resource in helping her Commanding Officer to handle *Cossack* in the fjord, and for distinguished service as Staff Officer (Operations) to Captain (D), Fourth Destroyer Flotilla.

Petty Officer Steward Rosario Asciak, H.M.S. *Cossack*;

Petty Officer Cook Dominick Spiteri, H.M.S. *Cossack*;

Petty Officer Steward Carmelo Sammut, H.M.S. *Cossack*;
for cheerful and ready work in caring for and feeding 55 Officers, prisoners released from *Altmark*.

INDEX

INDEX

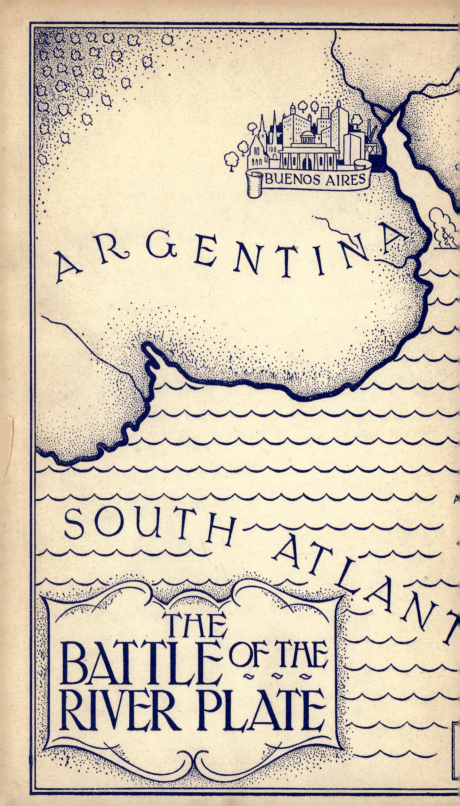